CAREERS in
NURSING

Options

VGM Professional Careers Series

NURSING

TERENCE J. SACKS

SECOND EDITION

VGM Career Books

Chicago   New York   San Francisco   Lisbon   London   Madrid   Mexico City
Milan   New Delhi   San Juan   Seoul   Singapore   Sydney   Toronto

Library of Congress Cataloging-in-Publication Data

Sacks, Terence J.
    Careers in nursing / Terence J. Sacks—2nd ed.
       p.   cm. — (VGM professional careers series)
    Includes bibliographical references.
    ISBN 0-07-140580-1
    1. Nursing—Vocational guidance.   I. Title.   II. VGM professional careers series.

RT82 .S23   2003
610'.73'06'9—dc21   2002034344

2 3 4 5 6 7 8 9 0   DOC/DOC   2 1 0 9 8 7 6 5 4

ISBN 0-07-140580-1

Interior design by Robert S. Tinnon

McGraw-Hill books are available at special quantity discounts to use as premiums and sales promotions, or for use in corporate training programs. For more information, please write to the Director of Special Sales, Professional Publishing, McGraw-Hill, Two Penn Plaza, New York, NY 10121-2298. Or contact your local bookstore.

This book is printed on acid-free paper.

CONTENTS

NURSING

CHAPTER

1

A LOOK AT THE FIELD

If you are reading this book, it is probably because you're interested in nursing and already know a little bit about it. Perhaps you know that a nurse is a licensed professional who is trained to care for sick people. True, but this definition is a little too general. For example, there are caretakers who take care of elderly people or those who are infirm—unable to take care of themselves—but these caretakers are not necessarily nurses. So what exactly is a nurse? One basic definition appeared in the September 1949 issue of the *American Journal of Nursing*, which said: "Nursing is the art of helping people feel better—as simple and complex as this." That's it—direct and to the point. Rosella Schlorfel, in the December 1973 issue of *Nursing Outlook*, offers a somewhat more detailed definition: "The nurse's primary intellectual concern and functions related thereto is that of helping each person attain his highest level of general health. The nurse's focus is on assessing people to regain health and the well or near-well to maintain or attain health through selective application of nursing science and the use of nursing strategies."

As you can see, the art/science of nursing is a complex one. We'll look more closely at what nurses do in Chapter 3, but for now let's concentrate on why you want to become a nurse. Perhaps you have watched nurses on TV and gotten the impression that nursing is a glamorous job with great pay. If that is the reason you want to be a nurse, forget it; nursing is not for you. Although the pay is not bad, nursing cannot be considered a glamorous job by any stretch of the imagination. One of the first tasks you will do as a new nurse is to bathe patients. And that's just the beginning. You'll also need to perform some less than desirable jobs such as emptying bedpans and cleansing patients of vomit and blood.

Or perhaps you think that studying medicine is too long and involved or too costly to pursue right now, and you want to do something else until you can get into medical school. Stop right there. Nursing is not for you. If you think of nursing as a stopgap until something better comes along, you likely won't last a day. Nursing is a highly demanding job, involving some very special skills in handling those who are sick, crippled, or diseased. This is not the kind of job that you can turn off and turn on. It'll take every bit of your skill, energy, and concern, and then some, to do properly.

Nurses assess signs and symptoms of their patients' health and react to them accordingly. This requires critical thinking, organizational skills, and capability in relating to patients, their families, and other health care professionals who may not always agree with you. It also requires your willingness to do the most menial and degrading work and to do it with good spirit, realizing that this is part of what is involved in caring for and restoring a sick patient to good health.

What else should you know about nursing in general? Well, for starters, registered nurses (R.N.s) are the largest part of the health care team. In 2000, for instance, there were about 2,696,000 licensed R.N.s in the United States, of whom nearly 82 percent were actively employed in the field. These figures are taken from the National Sample Survey of Registered Nurses, the largest and most extensive source of information on the nursing field. Here are some other interesting facts that the survey showed:

• 12.3 percent, or 333,000 of active licensed R.N.s, are from one or more racial or ethnic minority backgrounds. This was up considerably from the 246,363 of racial or ethnic minority backgrounds reported in 1996. Of these, 107,527 were African-American; 86,434 were Asian/Pacific Islanders; 40,559 were Latino; and 11,843 were listed as "other" in 1996.

• There has been a significant shift upward in the age of R.N.s over the years. In 1980, 52.9 percent of R.N.s were under the age of forty, but by 2000, only 31.7 were under forty.

• Although the total U.S. population increased 13.7 percent between 1990 and 2000, the number of nurses entering the workforce was just 4.1

percent higher between 1996 and 2000, down considerably from the 14.2 percent growth between 1992 and 1996.

• Men accounted for 5.9 percent of all R.N.s in 2000, up from 5.4 percent in 1996 and 4.3 percent in 1992.

The number of nurses working in hospitals went up slightly from 1,270,000 in 1996 to 1,300,323 in 2000.

• Of the 2,115,815 R.N.s employed in 1996, 58.4 percent had less than a bachelor's degree in preparing for a nursing career (502,959 had diplomas and 731,613 had an associate's degree in nursing). An estimated 672,914 (31.8 percent) of employed R.N.s had bachelor's degrees, 193,159 (9.1 percent) had master's degrees, and 14,300 (.6 percent) had doctorate degrees.

• Approximately 161,711 nurses, or 6.3 percent of all registered nurses in the United States in March of 1996, had the credentials to practice as what are known as "advanced practice nurses." These included 7,800 who were trained to practice in either of two categories of advanced practice nurses (APNs): clinical nurse specialists or nurse practitioners. Of the remaining APNs, almost 54,000 were clinical nurse specialists, 63,191 were nurse practitioners, 30,300 were nurse anesthetists, and 6,500 were nurse-midwives. See Chapter 3 for more information about advanced practice nurses.

• The overwhelming majority of registered nurses practiced in hospitals in 2000 (nearly 60 percent). Of the remainder who were working, 17 percent, or 362,648 R.N.s, worked as community or public health nurses and 8.5 percent, or about 179,000 R.N.s, worked in ambulatory care settings, including physicians' offices, health maintenance organizations, or solo or group practices. Nursing homes or other extended care facilities employed 170,856, or 8.1 percent of the total. The remaining employed R.N.s worked in areas such as nursing education, national or state offices of associations, or insurance companies.

You can see that nursing is quite a big field, accounting for more than half of the four million estimated to be working in health care. And that does not include licensed practical nurses (L.P.N.s), whose educational background is not as extensive as that of R.N.s (see Chapter 3).

But nursing is also quite varied. In the next section, you can read about some of the diverse duties and assignments of those involved in the general field of nursing.

NURSING PROFILES

Thirty-three-year-old Jennifer W., a nurse practitioner, takes care of children with infections and earaches and helps elderly patients control their diabetes and blood pressure. Jennifer works at a nursing center in a converted three-flat in Chicago's inner city Lawndale area, which suffers from a critical shortage of doctors. She and other advanced practice nurses (a broad term that includes nurse practitioners) are generally more willing to practice in poor urban areas where historically few doctors have wanted to practice. "I love my work," says Jennifer. "I enjoy being able to work out decisions about the care and treatment of the patients I see, young and old."

As a nurse practitioner, Jennifer can examine patients, make a diagnosis, and order drugs that do not require prescriptions. In addition, she does lots of patient teaching. In Illinois, nurse practitioners such as Jennifer work collaboratively with physicians. Nurse practitioners say that the care they provide is comparable to that of physicians, although they will refer the more complicated patients to physicians.

Sue H. loves her job as an orthopedic nurse at a large public hospital, the sole hospital for the city's poor people. However, at times she finds the work oppressive. "Why should a nurse have to make beds or empty bedpans?" she asks, thus pinpointing an area of friction for many nurses who feel put upon because many hospitals refuse to hire support help to make beds or empty urinals. "If you have to make eight beds and write nursing care plans, that's a big part of your time," she says. "Wouldn't it make more sense for me to use my skills in caring for patients who are really sick and leave the nitty-gritty details such as bedpan brigade to lesser-skilled personnel?"

Along the same lines, Suzy R. states: "If there was one nurse for every two patients, there'd be no care problem. But that's not the way it works. They split nursing into tasks, making the job task-oriented rather than letting us care for patients. I don't want to be known as a nurse who did her nursing plans, or her report on the narcotics cabinet, while all about her patients were dying.

"It's all defensive medicine. . . . You can't even treat a kidney cancer patient without having to write for an hour. You have to include biographical profiles, and these can go on for pages at a time. Almost half of your time is spent on paperwork when patients are admitted. Instead of making patients comfortable, you have to write them up. And with the limited time we have, should nurses be planning care or caring for patients?" Although she loves nursing, there are many aspects of nursing that make her bitter. Perhaps that explains why she is currently on leave from her job in the cardiac unit of a large hospital, uncertain of whether she wants to return.

Mickey E. not only provides well-baby care at a large metropolitan hospital, she delivers babies, too. Mickey is a certified nurse-midwife. Like Jennifer, the nurse practitioner described above, she's an advanced practice nurse. Such nurses—nurse practitioners, nurse-midwives, nurse anesthetists, and clinical nurse specialists—are all nurses, but by virtue of their training, they are able to handle many of the problems or cases formerly handled only by physicians, thus freeing the doctor to deal with the more complex or serious cases.

As a nurse-midwife, Mickey says that she can spend more time explaining health care and preventive treatment to her patients than doctors can. She points to a study that shows that a typical nurse-midwife spends half an hour speaking to patients, compared to the five minutes averaged by most physicians.

NURSING TODAY

After reading these profiles, you can see that nursing is infinitely varied. Although all nurses receive about the same training and have the same skills, there is quite a bit of difference in what they do, depending on where they work. Thus, a nurse in an intensive care unit (ICU) or in the emergency or operating room must have training and background in highly complex machinery and equipment. All of nursing is patient-oriented, but nurses in these fields have the added need of working with and understanding technologically sophisticated machines, such as the heart-lung machine in the operating room or the specialized equipment used to administer anesthesia to patients who are undergoing surgery. Multiply this by dozens of other pieces of equipment and you have some idea of what it is like to work in any one of these areas.

Then there are nurses who work in medical-surgical units ministering to the needs of patients who suffer from chronic diseases such as arthritis or diabetes or who are recovering from surgery. Nurses in these areas are much more likely to do hands-on nursing, such as taking temperature and other vital signs, drawing blood, taking pulse and blood pressure, and so forth.

Nursing itself is also highly specialized. Nurses in a hospital setting work in any one of many individualized units: emergency room (ER), operating and recovery room, obstetrics (labor and delivery nurses), neonatal areas (caring for newborns in the nursery), pediatrics (working with youngsters from about age two to adolescents or teenagers), and outpatient (working with patients who attend any of several clinics in medicine and surgery). These are just a few of the larger hospital units where you will find nurses. Additional units include orthopedics, psychiatry, pulmonary (for patients with lung diseases), ophthalmology (eye problems), and so forth. And the field is getting even more specialized as new technologies and treatments are unveiled and hospitals need nurses trained in these specific areas.

But hospitals, while still the largest employers of nurses (hospitals employ nearly 60 percent of all nurses) are not the "end all" for nursing. Nurses are also found in private duty, working in the homes of patients who require constant round-the-clock nursing care; in physicians' offices; in nursing homes; in clinics; in twenty-four-hour emergency care centers; in managed-care centers, where patients come in for routine checkups and inoculations and have their vital signs checked; and in other settings. There are also nurses who work in schools or in industrial complexes, where they may deal with patients suffering from various work-related illnesses, and those working in dialysis centers, community health centers, and so forth. The list goes on and on. But hospital nursing has been almost from the start and is still by far the largest employer of nurses and the place where most nurses receive their clinical training.

Any way you look at it, nursing, the profession that Florence Nightingale helped advance in the mid-nineteenth century, has changed radically in the past few decades. And it has changed in more ways than one. Not too many years ago, if you had walked into any hospital, you'd be likely to see nurses in starched white or striped uniforms patrolling the wards, with their nursing caps anchored tightly to their heads. In their white hose and stiff uniforms, nurses were indeed formidable no-nonsense caregivers not to be trifled with. Today the atmosphere in most hospitals is much more relaxed, and you are likely to find nurses wearing colorful smocks and contrasting pants and, most likely, no nursing caps. Some might argue that the starched nursing uniforms of past years added to the nurse's professionalism and image. Today, however, comfort and flexibility are key. Nurses contend that they are better able to care for patients and to negotiate the turns and twists of most hospitals in better shape and more quickly than the nurse of the past.

Nursing today is an entirely different kind of career than it was thirty years ago, or even ten or fifteen years ago. There are many forces at work—most of them beyond the nurse's control—that have thrown the majority of traditional practices and traditions into disarray.

Demand for Nurses

For many years following World War II and extending through the 1980s, nurses were in such short supply that hospitals throughout the country were offering handsome rewards in the form of round-trip vacations and bonuses for signing up. According to Gerry Merullo, then-executive director of the American Nurses Association, those boom days ended around 1994, and through 1997 hospitals were downsizing their nursing staffs and replacing nurses with less skilled, less costly nursing personnel. But today, because of increasingly complex technology and the demand for nurses to cope with the needs of sicker patients, R.N.s are once more at a premium in hospitals. The U.S. Department of Health and Human Resources sees the problem worsening dramatically in years to come.

Because of the anticipated demand for R.N.s in community health centers, home health care, and hospital care, the Bureau of Labor Statistics has listed nursing as one of the top forty growth jobs for the next ten years. It has projected a need for 2.6 million R.N.s by 2005, more than five hundred thousand R.N.s over current levels.

The picture of nursing staffing needs in hospitals is somewhat confusing. On the one hand, hospitals are treating ever-increasing numbers of patients on an outpatient basis and concentrating more on the extremely ill patients. At the same time, due to pressures of managed-care providers and various public health care programs, such as Medicare and Medicaid, to lower hospital costs, patients are being discharged much sooner than in the past. This means that patient care in hospitals today is more intense and complex than it has been, so that highly trained nurses—nurses who can act quickly on data from monitor screens and perhaps start lifesaving treatment, often without a physician at hand—are in great demand.

On the other hand, there is still the downsizing of hospital nursing staffs and reassignment of R.N. duties to lower-level nurses—licensed practical nurses and nurses' aides, for instance. Even so, it is anticipated that nurses with bachelor's degrees and above will be in great demand. According to the American Nurses Association, the current nurse staffing situation is a real threat to our entire health care system. "The nurse staffing crisis and the growing shortage of nurses are critical," says the ANA. "Employers are already having difficulty hiring experienced nurses—especially in emergency departments, critical care, labor and delivery, and long-term care." In addition, the potential impact of the war on terrorism on nurse staff vacancies—combined with the efforts to enhance our ability to respond to biological and chemical warfare—will place even greater strains on America's nurses, says the ANA.

Then, too, there is the fact that nurses who have at least a bachelor's degree will be eligible for advancement to supervisory and administrative positions. But it should be noted that in many cases, a master's degree in nursing or even higher would be required to qualify for these positions.

Advantages and Disadvantages

Despite all of these opposing pulls on the nursing staff, particularly as it pertains to hospital nursing staff needs, nursing remains a source of great satisfaction and joy to many nurses in practice today. Time after time, nurses comment that there is no greater satisfaction than the knowledge that they have contributed to the restoration of patients, many of them extremely sick, to full health. As a veteran nurse at a large teaching hospital put it, "There is nothing more satisfying than to receive the thanks and gratitude of a patient whom you have helped to full health after surgery or delivering a baby."

There are many other pluses in this field that make nursing highly desirable. For one, the pay is excellent. At the top of the pile, the National Sample Survey of Registered Nurses shows that in 2000, the average salary for full-time R.N.s had increased to $46,782 a year. On the lower end of the scale, *Nursing 2001*'s annual survey showed that new L.P.N.s earned $11.88 an hour while new R.N.s averaged $16.24 an hour.

The other obvious advantage offered by nursing is that jobs are available in almost all areas of the country. So if you'd like to move or if you have a partner who has been transferred to another part of the country, there is always the possibility of obtaining a nursing job in the area to which he or she has been assigned.

But there are disadvantages to nursing that should not be ignored. As has already been stated in this chapter, in an effort to reduce the nursing staff, hospitals often assign nurses to tasks that could be done by lower-level employees. There is also the very real possibility of losing your position due to hospital downsizing. And many nurses today are serving as managers, supervising the work of lower-level employees such as licensed practical nurses and nurses' aides. This can be a source of resentment or of optimism, depending upon your viewpoint. If you enjoy working hands-on with patients, this could be a real disappointment. On the other hand, if you like to supervise and be more involved in outpatient care plans and other administrative tasks, then perhaps you will find the trend toward more management of patients to your liking.

These are some of the more obvious pluses and minuses to take into account as you decide whether to pursue a career in nursing.

FACTORS THAT WILL IMPACT THE FUTURE OF NURSING

Let's take a brief look at some of the forces you can expect to shape the field of nursing in the near future. As has been shown, new methods of getting around costly hospital treatment—including downsizing of hospital staffs and reassignment of typical nursing duties to lower-level employees—have changed the picture of nursing completely. So what can we look forward to in the immediate future?

With people living much longer—the estimated population in 1994 was approximately 260 million, up from 236 million in 1985—the elderly require plenty of care for conditions that are often very costly and preventable. An estimated one out of every ten Americans is over sixty-five. And the eighty-five and older group is one that is growing the most rapidly. According to the U.S. Census Bureau, there are already more than one hundred thousand citizens who are one hundred years old or older. Nursing care in the home will increase, backed up by social services that are often coordinated by the nurse (who also handles patient follow-up). Since older patients are being discharged sooner, there will be considerably more call for care in nursing homes. Nurses for the elderly (geriatric nurses) and the highly trained advanced practice nurses (nurse practitioners) will be in great demand both to give care and to supervise care offered by less well-trained personnel.

Then, too, health care in hospital outpatient clinics and in settings outside of the hospital is already on the rise and can be expected to increase sharply in the future, as a means of avoiding more costly hospital inpatient care whenever possible. Although nearly 60 percent of all nurses still work in hospitals, this figure is expected to shrink considerably in the near future, and the slack in employment will be taken up by, among others, community health centers (numbering about 250 in 1992). In many cases these centers are staffed and managed by nurses and serve persons of all ages, income groups, and ethnic backgrounds. Many are affiliated with universities, so that faculty and students provide much of the care.

Yet another rapidly growing setting for health care of all kinds, including nursing, is the home. Here you not only provide care but, along with professionals, therapists, nutritionists, and others, you teach patients how to care for themselves—how to administer diabetes injections, for instance, or how to get around if you have prostheses (artificial limbs). This involves using equipment that at one time you would have seen only in the hospital: respirators, drainage pumps, IV (intravenous) lines to deliver drugs and food to patients, and the like. In addition, community health nurses often care for mental patients or take part in improving the quality of life for the terminally ill in their own homes.

Some nursing personnel will be cut back in hospitals due to budgetary considerations, but nurses who are highly trained will still be in demand. As stated earlier, hospitals are presently concentrating on patients who are extremely ill. Consequently, hospital patient care is increasingly intense and complex, calling for nurses with special training and skills to care for these very sick patients.

Lifestyle, which can be increasingly frantic and fast-paced, is another factor that demands adequate nursing support. Nurses are now needed to work with business and industry in helping employers to cope with employee stress, which can result in physical and emotional breakdown. Often nurses are called on to teach employees about the effects of overwork, anxiety, and tension.

And the plain truth is that many nurses themselves can burn out from high levels of stress. As we have seen, nurses are often called on to care for more and more patients, to perform menial chores that could be handled by less well-trained employees, and, in some cases, to work with equipment that is outdated or inadequate. In other words, they may have the responsibility, but they do not have the means of handling ever more patients. And although there are measures the nurse can take to prevent such burnout, emotional stress is often a condition of hospital nursing, and it can be expected to increase in the future, thus creating yet another source of nursing manpower needs.

A large part of the nursing manpower dilemma will be addressed by advanced practice nurses—nurse practitioners, nurse-midwives, nurse anesthetists, and clinical nurse specialists. These highly trained and well-qualified advanced practice nurses—who, as some estimate, can provide 80 percent of primary medical care as well as physicians can, and do it at a lower cost—will play an ever-increasing role in nursing care in all settings: the home, the community health center, and managed-care (health maintenance organizations), among others.

Although there are parts of the nursing career equation that might cause some concern, overall the picture is bright for those who enjoy working with people and who are willing to work hard. In chapters to come, we will trace the history of nursing (Chapter 2); look at where the jobs are and what nurses do (Chapter 3); show you how to decide if nursing is for you (Chapter 4); find out how to get into nursing school, take a look at the prerequisites, and learn how to finance a nursing education (Chapter 5); find out how to get started, locate sources of jobs, and learn how to advance in the profession (Chapter 6); and, finally, look at the future of nursing (Chapter 7). Chapter 8 features conversations with those in the profession—nursing practitioners, advanced practice nurses, students, and nursing school administrators.

C H A P T E R

NURSING THROUGH THE AGES

Nursing, as we know it today, descends from the work of Florence Nightingale, perhaps the world's most famous nurse. During the 1850s she defined the nature of nursing and identified both who and what a nurse should be. Prior to that time, nursing existed, but treatment was administered according to the beliefs of the time, and, for the most part, was assumed by women who had no formal training.

HISTORY OF NURSING

In all likelihood some form of nursing has existed since earliest recorded history. Recently found documents in Babylon and Egypt refer to nursing care given primarily by women.

In the early era of Christianity, a group of wealthy women known as deaconesses established hospitals for the ill and took care of the sick. But during the Middle Ages the Church suppressed such unregulated activity, and the care of the sick was taken over by orders of monks and nuns and groups of laymen, who organized to form lay orders, with nursing as their primary activity. At the conclusion of the Crusades, a military male nursing order, the Knights Hospitallers, was formed.

By the end of the Middle Ages, hospitals staffed primarily by nuns existed all over Europe. But the care offered was poor and extremely limited. Male nurses, except for a few religious orders, almost disappeared from the scene—the result of the growth of Catholic and Protestant orders of female nurses.

Then, as the Reformation in the sixteenth century approached, with its emphasis on practical living and science, service to the sick took a sharp turn for the worse. Protestant leaders called for the employment of nurse deaconesses to care for the sick. But with the reemphasis on religion and on charitable work, noblewomen of humanitarian concern no longer felt the need to provide nursing care. A few hospitals attempted to establish a higher standard of care, but overall conditions were deplorable and the work was not considered fit for respectable women. Consequently the task of providing care in hospitals fell to women of low educational background and standing. These women may not have been able to live up to the standards characterized by the French philosopher Diderot, when he said that nurses should be "patient, mild, and compassionate" and should "console the sick, foresee their needs, and relieve their tedium."

So things stood until the era of St. Vincent DePaul, a parish priest whose lifetime of work is considered the birth of modern nursing. It was St. Vincent DePaul who organized the Sisters of Charity, who to this day run some of the finest hospitals in existence. The desperate plight of the sick affected him deeply, and he spent his entire life attempting to better theirs. Under the able supervision of Louise de Marillac, a close follower of St. Vincent, the order of the Sisters of Charity was formed in Paris in 1633. Throughout history, this order has served as one of the most widely disseminated of all charitable orders. Particularly noteworthy was the order's work in the Napoleonic and Crimean Wars.

Some two hundred years later and prior to the revolutionary work of Florence Nightingale, Theodore Fliedner, an Evangelical pastor, opened a small hospital with his wife in 1833. Located at Kaiserswerth on the Rhine, it was staffed by a group of carefully selected young women, also known as deaconesses. From this core group, the deaconesses branched out into hundreds of groups, performing their nursing duties with kindness and expertise.

Florence Nightingale

Among those exposed to the high quality of care given at the Kaiserswerth hospital was a young Englishwoman of wealthy background and social standing, Florence Nightingale. According to one description of the care given at that period was this account taken from the May 1970 issue of *R.N. Magazine*:

> Hospitals of that day were dumping grounds for the poor. Surgery . . . combined risk with torture, for anesthesia was not yet in use. Sanitation was unknown and patients were seldom bathed or bed linens changed. Infections often killed more patients than did the diseases that brought the patients to the hospital in the first place.

Against this background of ignorance and deplorable hospital conditions, Florence Nightingale vowed to do something to right the situation. Because of her standing in society, she had access to some of the prominent people of the time. Following her visit to Pastor Fliedner's Kaiserswerth hospital and against her family's wishes, in 1853 she became superintendent of the Institution for Sick Gentlewomen in Distressed Circumstances in London.

But it was her historic work in caring for the sick and hospitalized during the Crimean War that primarily made her name a byword in nursing. In 1854 the English secretary of state, an old-time friend, asked her to lead a group of nurses to the Crimea at government expense. And so, with thirty-eight carefully selected nurses in hand, she arrived at Scutari in the Turkish Crimean Peninsula, only to find that the army doctors and surgeons were unwilling to accept her services. However, after disease and more fighting in that disastrous conflict threatened the collapse of the British units, the doctors were forced to ask for Nightingale's help. They did not have to ask twice. Quickly she had the filthy hospital at Scutari cleaned up, used her own supplies to feed the soldiers, ordered camp followers to wash their clothes, eradicated the hordes of vermin, and offered the suffering soldiers decent care. War correspondents wrote dispatches to their home newspapers of the "ministering angel," and Nightingale's reputation spread worldwide.

With her fame established and funds pouring in, Nightingale opened the first school for the training of nurses at St. Thomas's Hospital in London. The program offered classes for both medical school physicians and teaching sisters. Soon the "Nightingale nurses," as they came to be known, with their vast nursing expertise, were in great demand.

In response to need, Nightingale sent school graduates to other hospitals all over the world, including British hospitals in India, to train other nurses. Through her volumes of written works, she helped to reform hospital care, workhouses, and the army medical department. She also established two missions for modern nursing care for the sick. To get some idea of Nightingale's impact on modern nursing care, you need only consider these words taken from her 1859 book *Notes on Nursing: What It Is and What It Is Not*.

> It has been limited to signify little more than the administration of medicines and the application of poultices. It ought to signify the proper use of fresh air, light, warmth and administration of diet— all at the least expense to the vital power of the patients.

Clearly Nightingale was years ahead of her time in defining the scope and role of nursing in health care.

Clara Barton

Meanwhile the onset of the Civil War in 1861 saw the wounded of both sides cared for by a variety of persons of all stations of life—high and low. Included in this force were nuns, untrained nurses, others employed by the army, and so-called camp followers. In the Northern nursing ranks were women of wealth who later helped establish nursing training schools. Notable among those providing care for the many thousands of sick and wounded was Clara Barton, who came to be known as the "angel of the battlefield" for her heroism and concern in ministering to the needs of the fallen soldiers. Barely five feet tall, she began work among homesick troops from her native state of Massachusetts by collecting and distributing brandy and tobacco, lemons, soaps, sewing kits, and homemade jellies.

Following the bloody battle of Bull Run, she knew that more help was needed and she remained behind the lines, realizing that her place was "anywhere between the bullet and the battlefield." She followed the fighting, brewing gruel over open fires to feed the sick, dispensing bandages and kind words, and sometimes digging bullets out of the flesh of victims with a penknife. She was all over the battle lines—at Cedar Mountain, Second Bull Run, Chantilly, South Mountain, and Antietam.

When Southern cannons threatened to hit field hospitals and male assistants scurried for cover, she held her ground, holding the rolling operating table steady so the surgeon could work. A surgeon who witnessed her heroism said of Barton: "In my feeble estimation, General McClellan, with all of his laurels, sinks into insignificance beside the true heroine of the time, the angel of the battlefield."

Nearly half a million men lost their lives in the Civil War. Soldiers on both sides suffered cruelly from their wounds, which often were infected. They also suffered from frostbite, as well as many other ills brought on by malnutrition, exposure, and lack of sanitation. More than three thousand women, nearly all without training, volunteered to care for the sick and wounded.

After the war Barton took her nursing skills to Europe during the Franco-Prussian War. She later helped to found the American Red Cross.

Schools

Few of the schools founded after the Civil War followed the educational model established by Florence Nightingale. Other than a night supervisor, operating room supervisor, and nursing superintendent, students—a source of cheap labor—provided all care.

The period directly following the Civil War saw the establishment of the first schools to train nurses: the Bellevue School in New York, generally credited as being the first; the Boston Training School for Nurses, which later became the Massachusetts General Hospital School of Nursing; and the Connecticut Training School in New Haven.

Other Prominent Women

Several of the women who came to the fore after the Civil War included Helen Bowden, one of a forceful, vital group of women who wanted to clean up the slovenliness and filth that characterized hospitals. During her years as "lady superintendent" at Bellevue, she put the hospital in first-class shape and strengthened the standing of the nursing school.

Linda Richards, "America's first trained nurse," was awarded the first graduate nurse diploma from the New England Hospital for Women and Children in 1873 and went on to become night supervisor at Bellevue. She played a leading role in the organization of at least twelve nursing schools, all based on the Nightingale system of nursing.

Still later, Lillian Wald achieved fame as a pioneer of visiting nurse societies. In 1893 she founded the Henry Street Settlement for social work, which she later expanded to include a public health nursing center. She took a leading role in establishing the U.S. Children's Bureau in 1912 and was influential, along with Clara Barton, in the establishment of the American Red Cross.

Yet another name prominent in the development of the profession was Isabel Robb, the first principal at the nursing school of the famed Johns Hopkins Hospital in Baltimore. She is perhaps best known as the first nurse in the country to propose and promote the idea of a national nurses association, and after the establishment of the American Nurses Association was elected its first president in 1896.

World War I

World War I was another brutal conflict in which hardship, injury, illness, and infection caused the deaths of hundreds of thousands of soldiers on both sides of the war. Before it ended in 1918, some fifty thousand nurses served overseas, many of them members of Red Cross–based hospital units.

One legendary nurse forever immortalized in World War I was Edith Cavell, an English nurse whose tragic death made her a martyr. She was killed as a result of her activities while in charge of a hospital in Brussels, Belgium, when German troops occupied the city in 1915. Nurse Cavell was involved for several months in helping two hundred Allied soldiers escape to Holland. Arrested by the Germans, she was sentenced to death after she admitted her activities. "Patriotism is not enough," she is said to have exclaimed as she stood before the firing squad. Her body was later removed to Norwich, England, her birthplace, where a monument was erected in her memory. Mt. Edith Cavell in Jasper National Park, in Alberta, Canada, is named in her honor.

Following the war, nurses were deeply involved in caring for what is widely regarded as the worst epidemic the world has ever known, the Spanish influenza, or flu. The number of people who died from it is put conservatively at twenty million, more than a half million in the United States alone.

The Depression and World War II

Like nearly everyone else, nurses strongly felt the effects of the Depression of the 1930s, and many lost their jobs in that period. Nursing schools and hospitals closed, along with factories and many corporate offices. And the situation remained largely unchanged until the outbreak of World War II. With the need for trained nurses widely recognized, in 1943 Congress authorized the awarding of stipends, uniforms, and scholarships for more than 170,000 anticipated nurses. Of these, some 75,000 served in the armed forces in almost every theater of the war, many with great valor and distinction.

MODERN NURSING

After World War II ended, many nurses used the GI Bill of Rights to advance their education. Some of the nurses who had earned bachelor's or master's degrees, to their credit, used these degrees to become leaders in psychiatric, public health, and operating room nursing. This, in turn, set off the trend toward obtaining even higher degrees in nursing and, eventually, the development of specialized practices in nursing (see Chapter 3). It also spotlighted the need for professional organization of the field.

Nursing Associations

In 1952 six then-existing nursing organizations were merged into two—the American Nurses Association (ANA) and the National League for Nursing. The ANA has always concerned itself primarily with defining the functions, standards, and qualifications of nursing and with improvement in job security for nurses in areas such as salaries, working conditions, and benefits. It is comprised of state and local chapters. Members must be registered nurses. The National League for Nursing, a more consumer-oriented group, has focused primarily on accreditation and upgrading of nursing education standards at all levels. Its members include nurses, persons from other health professions, and interested citizens.

In 1965 the ANA published a position paper calling for nursing education to be offered only in institutions of higher education. As a result, many diploma schools in existence prior to the end of the nineteenth century were closed. In the intervening years this trend has continued.

In the position paper, the ANA also called for all nursing education to take place in colleges and universities. Recommended in the paper were the establishment of two levels of nursing practice: professional and technical. The professional nurse would have the bachelor's or higher degree, while the technical nurse would have an associate's degree (obtained in a two-year nursing program offered primarily in junior or community colleges) and work under the supervision of the professional nurse.

The specific duties of various types of nurses are discussed in the following chapter. For more information about the educational requirements of the different levels of nursing, see Chapter 5.

CHAPTER 3

WHAT DO NURSES DO?

To a great extent, what nurses do depends on where they are employed. But there are some common duties that apply to nearly all nurses, regardless of where they work.

1. Nurses care for the sick and maimed and help people to stay well. Typically they are concerned with the "whole" person—they work not just with the patient's physical well-being, but with his or her mental and emotional needs as well.

2. Nurses observe, evaluate, and record symptoms, reactions, and progress of patients resulting from various medications, treatments or therapies, surgeries, or nutrition received. In working with physicians to assess how patients are doing, they listen to breathing sounds, check heart rates, and measure blood pressure. They interpret laboratory tests, separating normal from abnormal functions. With their knowledge of drugs, they can help to teach patients about medications, dosages, possible side effects, and intended results. As part of the health care team, nurses work with physicians and others during treatments and examinations. They give medications and help patients during convalescence and rehabilitation.

3. Nurses develop and manage nursing care plans; familiarize patients and their families with proper care; and work to help sick people, individually or in groups, doing what is required to improve or maintain their health.

The general parameters or rules as to what nurses can and cannot do are governed by state laws; but it is the work setting—where nurses physically work—that determines to a great extent what nurses can do.

HOSPITALS

Hospitals are still the major place of employment for nearly 60 percent of all nurses. Most hospital nurses are staff nurses who provide bedside care for patients and carry out the doctor's orders. They may also supervise licensed practical nurses and aides. With the continued advances in technology, the staff nurse usually has the opportunity to handle a wide variety of cases.

In general, hospitals now offer care in specialty areas, such as kidney dialysis, where patients whose kidneys are not functioning can dispose of wastes through the use of artificial kidney machines. Or they may work in various kinds of intensive care units such as cardiac or neurological, each with its own special equipment that nurses will have to understand or be trained to use.

A new staff nurse should expect to undergo an initial orientation period, during which time the policies and procedures of the hospital and its philosophy of nursing care are taught. In addition, he or she will learn about the routine of each of the three daily nursing shifts that most hospitals operate on.

The Emergency Room (ER)

Sick or injured patients of all ages can be brought or come in to the emergency room on their own. The police or paramedics bring in other, more seriously ill patients. In the ER, the nurse will triage: that is, evaluate the seriousness of a patient's condition. Patients may be suffering from various traumas such as broken bones, cuts and abrasions, gunshot wounds, serious burns, heart attacks, strokes, and so on. Other patients come in with serious respiratory illnesses, asthmatic attacks, strokes, and high fevers.

Intensive Care Unit (ICU) or Cardiac Care Unit (CCU)

Critically ill patients requiring more intensive, one-on-one nursing care are brought to this unit. Patients may suffer from a variety of serious ailments, such as stroke, diabetes, blood loss from serious car or home accidents, or dysfunction of organs such as the kidney or liver, and so forth.

Medical-Surgical

Patients suffering from a variety of medical and surgical ailments, ranging from back to eye surgery and from stomach to swallowing disorders, are cared for here, usually in private rooms, either by staff nurses or by licensed practical nurses or nurses' aides working under the supervision of the staff nurse.

Obstetrics and Gynecology

In this area, nurses work with women who come in to deliver their babies. They also may be assigned to the nursery for the care of the newborn. In many cases a neonatal intensive unit may be attached for the care of premature infants, who may require special breathing equipment or whose hearts or digestive systems may not be fully functional.

Women are also admitted to this area for surgery and for treatment of other medical conditions.

The Operating Room (OR)

Staff nurses, working with the supervising physicians, anesthetists, and other OR personnel, are involved in surgeries ranging from removal of gallstones to complex eye or heart surgery.

Operating room nurses also may be required to work with surgeons who provide laser surgery or those who do microsurgery, working with equipment that enables the surgeon to operate, for example, on a microscopic area of the spine.

Outpatient or Ambulatory Care/Clinics

Patients not sick enough to be admitted to the hospital come in as outpatients for minor treatments, removal of bandages, or for follow-up to surgeries of various kinds.

Other common hospital units to which nurses are assigned include pediatrics (involving children two years of age through adolescence), orthopedics (for patients suffering from broken bones, torn ligaments, back problems, and the like), and psychiatry (working with patients who have emotional and mental problems). In other cases, hospitals may have special units for diabetes patients, pain control, or patients requiring eye care or surgery.

With additional training and the required educational background, nurses might also work in nursing administration—supervising the employment, training, and evaluation of nursing personnel—or they might be in-service educators, instructing nursing personnel in various new techniques or in hospital policies.

Head Nurse

Head nurses plan work schedules and assign nursing duties to nurses and aides in the care unit area. They train nurses and observe them in their patient care duties. They also make sure that adequate records are kept and that equipment and supplies are ordered as needed.

OTHER MAJOR WORK SETTINGS

There are a number of settings outside of the hospital where nurses are employed. Among the more common are the following:

Offices

Nurses assist physicians in private practice, clinics, surgicenters, emergency medical facilities, and health maintenance organizations (HMOs). They may be called on to prepare patients or to help out with patient examinations, handle medications and injections, dress wounds or surgical incisions, assist with minor surgery, and maintain records. In some cases the office nurse might be required to handle routine lab and office work or to act as a receptionist.

Private Homes

One of the fastest-growing branches of nursing is that of the private duty nurse. Home health care nurses provide care for patients in their homes, as prescribed by the physician. They may be employed by a private agency or a hospital. In this area, unlike in hospital nursing, private duty nurses would be largely on their own, experienced enough to render care for just about any patient who might be an invalid or housebound. They may be called on to care for and instruct patients—diabetics, for instance, on how to properly administer insulin, or how to apply dressings for patients recovering from an infection or surgery.

Patients needing home care cover the spectrum of recovering patients, including those recovering from illnesses and accident injuries, cancer, or childbirth. Private duty nurses must be able to work independently.

Nursing Homes

Working in a nursing home involves caring for patients who are elderly and/or have chronic conditions such as arthritis, diabetes, or heart problems. Patients needing care run the gamut from those suffering from Alzheimer's disease to those who have fractures. Although many tasks might be administrative and supervisory in nature, nursing home staff would also evaluate patients' conditions, develop plans for treatment, and supervise other nursing personnel—including nurses' aides and licensed practical nurses, who handle the more complex procedures such as starting intravenous solutions. Nurses might also work in specialty facilities for the care of long-term inpatients recovering from stroke or head injuries.

Public Health

Public health, one of the fastest-growing areas of nursing, offers many excellent opportunities for qualified R.N.s. Public health nurses work primarily with government or private agencies, such as the Visiting Nurse Association, or with a city health department. Their clients would include adults, children, and their families. They might work on disease prevention, nutrition, health education, and sanitation. Other duties might include arranging for immunizations, doing blood pressure testing, and checking vital signs. Most likely the public health nurse would work with teachers, community leaders, parents, physicians, and other health care workers in providing health care.

Industrial or Occupational Health

Nurses working in industrial or occupational health provide nursing care to workers with minor injuries, illnesses, or health complaints at the work site. They handle emergency care, prepare accident reports, and arrange for any necessary follow-up care. In addition to offering health counseling, these nurses assist with health examinations and inoculations and work out accident prevention programs.

Schools

School nurses provide services within the school for any health problems that might involve students or faculty. This job is particularly appealing to nurses who have school-age children, as their work hours and vacation time will be the same. School nurses are responsible for advising teachers of symptoms of illness and for alerting parents about possible or actual health problems, including below-normal hearing scores. They are also required to record and monitor immunizations and to participate in the prevention of communicable diseases. In addition to being licensed as a registered nurse, school nurses must meet any additional state or local school requirements.

The Armed Forces

Each of the nation's armed forces maintains its own nursing corps. Nurses working for the military provide direct patient care and may be involved in teaching, in-service education, and consulting with other government personnel—either in the continental United States or in any other part of the world where American troops or personnel are stationed.

Physical requirements for each branch vary somewhat, as do the educational requirements. For instance, the army corps will accept a nurse with a bachelor's degree from any accredited nursing school program, while the air corps will accept graduates of two-year nursing programs if they have at least three years of nursing experience. A nurse in the armed forces must be licensed as an R.N., be a citizen of the United States, and have proper letters of recommendation.

In addition to the openings in the armed forces, the Peace Corps, started by President Kennedy in 1961, accepts applications from registered nurses who are citizens of the United States. Other requirements include three years of nursing experience, a valid driver's license, and passing a rigorous physical. As U.S. representatives assigned to help promote peace in distant countries throughout the world, prospective Peace Corps nurses are carefully screened and undergo training for overseas duty, including language instruction in the country to which they are assigned. Duties might include nursing other Peace Corps volunteers, planning and putting into effect health care, and teaching natives in towns and villages and in local clinics or hospitals about health care techniques.

TYPES OF NURSES

Depending on their training, nurses can assume a variety of duties and responsibilities. Some of the more typical areas found in nursing include the following:

Advanced Practice Nurses

There are four categories of advanced practice nurses: nurse practitioners, certified nurse-midwives, clinical nurse specialists or nurse clinicians, and nurse anesthetists. Advanced practice nurses are registered nurses who by virtue of their training over and above that received by R.N.s are qualified to handle certain duties formerly restricted to physicians. These include prescribing medications (in all states), giving health examinations, and handling case histories. Advanced practice nurses can handle a wide range of health problems, usually working together with physicians, but in some cases independently. In all cases, what they are allowed to do in each classification is described in the medical practice acts for each state. The duties vary considerably from category to category, as do the qualifications and training required.

Specific duties are determined by specialty. For example, nurse practitioners conduct physical exams, take patient histories, diagnose and treat minor illness, order tests, and so forth. This nursing group, a relatively recent addition to the American health care scene, continues to grow and develop. Basic duties of each of the advanced practice nursing specialties are as follows:

Nurse Practitioner (NP)

There are approximately fifty thousand nurse practitioners working in various settings: clinics, nursing homes, hospitals, or in their own offices. Nurse practitioners are qualified to handle a wide range of health problems, and on the job they typically conduct physical exams, take case histories, diagnose and treat common minor injuries or illnesses, order and interpret lab and x-ray results, and counsel and educate patients. In all fifty states, NPs can prescribe medication. In some states they can work as independent practitioners; or they may work for a hospital, for a health maintenance organization, or in private industry.

Nurse practitioners date back to the early 1960s when Loretta Ford, R.N., and Henry Silver, M.D., established the first NP program in the area of pediatrics at the University of Colorado. Their goal, simply stated, was to prove that pediatric care could be delivered safely and inexpensively to patients in underserved areas of the country by nurses with specialized training. That and another pioneer program started at Duke University in 1965 were organized partially in response to the acute shortage of physicians and as a means of taking advantage of the influx of former corpsmen who hoped to utilize their training and experience in medicine to help fill the void in medical practitioners. Those involved in these first NP programs believed that NPs could handle many of the time-consuming tasks previously restricted to physicians, thus freeing up the physician to handle the more complex cases.

For the next ten years or so, certificate NP programs sprang up all over the country, each program with courses of varying lengths and prerequisites. Some programs required only an associate's (two-year nursing) degree and six months of nursing experience to qualify for a certificate. Later the federal government, in an effort to standardize NP programs, started to withhold funds to certificate programs and increase funding for master's degree programs. Today, most NP programs require the master's degree.

Although the aim in most NP programs was originally to provide primary "well care" and health maintenance, NP programs are now moving toward managing acute care as well as chronic illnesses, such as diabetes and heart disease. And NPs are practicing in new settings such as caring for hospital inpatients. Many NPs are likely to specialize in areas such as family planning, pediatrics, or working with the elderly.

One leading NP enthusiast, Maureen McCausland, vice president of nursing at Mt. Sinai Medical Center in New York, sees NPs in acute care practice. "NPs are very, very important as we advance toward the rapid changes in the health care field," she says. "Their role is much broader than that of simply replacing house officers as some have suggested. . . . They can provide continuity of care, expertise in discharge planning, and patient education and can help to reduce length of stays."

According to the National Sample Survey of Registered Nurses, NPs were more likely to provide preventive services than physicians were and about as likely to provide medications. Also, while the use of NPs is not common in private practice, it is much more customary at many large clinics run by HMOs.

Certified Nurse-Midwife (CNM)

Seven thousand certified nurse-midwives provide well-woman gynecological exams and handle low-risk prenatal (prebirth) labor and delivery and postdelivery care in the United States. In 1990 CNMs delivered 148,728 babies, or about 3.6 percent of all U.S. births, in hospitals, birth centers, and homes. About 5,700 are licensed to practice in all fifty states, as well as in many developing countries. They also handle postdelivery care for many new mothers and assist with family planning.

Certified nurse-midwives have been attending births in this country since colonial times. But the profession was not formally organized until the early 1920s, in response to an alarming rise in infant and maternal deaths in the United States. At that time, the Children's Bureau reported that 124 babies per one thousand were dying, and the number of maternal deaths was equally alarming.

CNMs must pass a national exam for certification administered by the American College of Nurse-Midwives. They must be R.N.s and graduates of an educational program accredited by the American College of Nurse-Midwives.

Clinical Nurse Specialist (CNS)

Approximately 58,000 clinical nurse specialists work in a variety of health settings: hospitals, clinics, nursing homes, their own offices, industry, home care, and HMOs. The CNS is qualified to handle a wide range of physical and mental health problems. Like nurse practitioners, they are qualified to do health assessments, make diagnoses, and give treatment. In addition to delivering patient care, they might also work as consultants or in research, education, and administration; or they might specialize in areas such as mental health, gerontology (medical problems of the elderly), cardiac or cancer care, and community or neonatal health.

Until fairly recently the clinical nurse specialist was trained to serve primarily as a consultant or resource person for staff education, while the NP received more training in patient care. But today these distinctions are often blurred, and there is discussion of merging the two groups together under the NP banner, and having most graduate nursing programs simply offer advanced nursing degrees.

Certified Registered Nurse Anesthetist (CRNA)

About twenty-eight thousand CRNAs work in this advanced nursing specialty, providing more than 65 percent of all anesthetics given to patients each year. They are the sole anesthesia providers in an estimated two-thirds of all rural hospitals, enabling these health care facilities to provide obstetrical, surgical, and trauma stabilization services.

CRNAs are involved in all phases of a patient's anesthesia care, monitoring the patient throughout the surgery regardless of whether the CRNA is working with a physician anesthesiologist or independently. CRNAs are qualified to provide every type of anesthetic in every setting in which anesthesia care is delivered in the United States. They work with the latest technology and anesthetics, enjoy maximum earning potential, can look forward to increased employment opportunities in a growing field, and have a high degree of autonomy.

Nurse anesthetists are credited with being the first profession to provide anesthesia services in the United States. As such, they are the oldest recognized category of advanced practice nurses. Nurse anesthetists were on hand providing anesthetic support for surgeries performed around the turn of the century, while medical schools did not provide formal training in anesthesia until the 1930s.

CRNAs practice with a high degree of autonomy. They carry a heavy load of responsibility and are compensated accordingly. Approximately 44 percent of the nation's twenty-eight thousand CRNAs are men, versus approximately 5 percent of the nursing profession as a whole.

CRNAs practice in every setting in which anesthesia is delivered: traditional hospital surgical suites and obstetrical delivery rooms; critical access hospitals; ambulatory surgical centers; the offices of dentists, podiatrists, ophthalmologists, and plastic surgeons; and U.S. military, public health services, and Veterans Administration health care facilities.

CRNAs are required to obtain forty hours of continuing education every two years to maintain their certification.

Licensed Practical Nurses

These nurses, numbering about seven hundred thousand, are in a category of their own. Known as licensed vocational nurses (L.V.N.s) in California and Texas, these nurses, like R.N.s, care for the sick, injured, and convalescing patients under the direction of physicians and R.N.s.

Licensed practical nurses provide basic bed care and take vital signs, such as blood pressure, pulse, and temperature. They also give injections and enemas, treat bedsores, dress wounds or sores, give alcohol rubs and massages, apply ice packs and hot water bottles, and insert catheters.

L.P.N.s observe patients and report negative reactions to medications or treatments. Most likely they would collect urine or feces samples for testing and perform routine lab tests. Like most nurses, licensed practical nurses help patients with bathing, feeding themselves, and personal hygiene. They also record food and liquid intake and output, and try to keep patients comfortable. In certain states where the law allows it, L.P.N.s may administer medications and start intravenous (IV) fluids, either for nutrition or medication. And in some states, they help deliver, care for, and feed infants.

In a nursing home, in addition to providing routine bed care, L.P.N.s might also help evaluate residents' needs, develop patient care plans, and supervise nurses' aides. In doctors' offices, they might be asked to make appointments, keep records, and handle other clerical duties. In a private home, they might be required to prepare meals and to instruct family members on simple nursing tasks.

This list of nursing specialties and duties is by no means complete because nursing, like medicine, is evolving. Every year new nursing specialties are emerging, each with its own requirements for practice and for certification. In other words, nursing is a growing, dynamic profession that is constantly changing. It involves a concentrated effort to keep up with the demands being made on practitioners in the face of new technology and new methods of health care delivery.

To get some idea of how nursing has advanced, you need only consider the duties of the student nurse in 1855, as enumerated in Keville Frederickson's excellent book, *Opportunities in Nursing Careers*:

- dress blisters, burns, sores, and wounds and apply poultices and minor dressings
- apply leeches, externally or internally
- administer enemas for men and women
- manage trusses and appliances of uterine complaints
- use the best method of friction to the body and to extremities
- manage helpless patients—moving, changing, personal cleanliness of, feeding, keeping warm, preventing and dressing bedsores
- bandage, make bandages and rollers, and line splints
- make beds and remove sheets while patient is still in bed
- cook gruel, arrowroot or egg flip, puddings, drinks, and so forth

In addition, nurses were expected to work exceptionally long hours for low pay. It was not unusual to have to work twelve hours a day, six days a week, earning enough money to cover only the rent and buy food. And if there was any money left over, you were expected to contribute it to charity.

Nurse's Aide

The nurse's aide, who is another member of the nursing team, performs the more routine duties of nursing, such as bathing and feeding patients and transporting them to various departments. This work does not require any post–high school education or licensure, so it is not covered in this book, but it should be noted that nurses' aides are being assigned an increasing number of tasks, as many R.N.s are phased out of hospital work for financial or budgetary reasons. These workers and the tasks they perform are assigned under the supervision of R.N.s.

NURSING DEMOGRAPHICS

To give you more of an idea of who nurses are and what they do, here are some facts compiled by the American Nurses Association:

1. **Gender.** Traditionally more women than men have chosen nursing as a profession, but the figures are changing. In 1996 only 5.4 percent of R.N.s working as nurses were men, but even this low figure represents a more-than-100-percent increase from 1990 in the number of men entering the profession.

2. **Racial/ethnic background.** Ninety percent of all nurses are Caucasian. About 10 percent of the employed R.N.s are of non-Caucasian backgrounds, including African-Americans, who make up 107,527, or 4 percent, of the nursing population; Asian or Pacific Islanders, who account for 40,559, or 1.6 percent, of all R.N.s; and Latinos, at 11,843, or .5 percent.

3. **Age.** The average age of all R.N.s was 44.3 years in 1996. About 58.4 percent had less than a bachelor's degree, while those with master's degrees totaled 9.1 percent. Twenty-seven percent had majored in liberal arts and 24 percent in health-related fields.

4. **Family status.** A majority—72 percent—of R.N.s are married; 17 percent are widowed, divorced, or separated; and the rest are single. More than half—55 percent—have children living at home, and 21 percent have children under six years old.

5. **Second-career R.N.** A large portion of R.N.s, almost 30 percent, has worked in a health care occupation before entering nursing school. About 65 percent had worked as nurses' aides and 29 percent as licensed practical nurses, showing that there is high upward mobility from L.P.N. to R.N.

6. **Degree status.** About 8 percent of those in the second-career category had post–high school degrees; more than half had their bachelor's degrees and almost 27 percent had majored in liberal arts.

SOME NURSE PROFILES

Before we look at some nurse profiles, keep in mind that nurses do not operate in a vacuum. They are members of the health care team and see to the implementation of the doctor's orders, both as to medications and other treatments.

However, despite the fact that they report to the attending physician, nurses are not puppets. Mistakes happen, and if the physician writes an order for the wrong medication or the dosage is incorrect, a nurse should know enough about medications and their uses to catch the mistake. Nurses are a part of the health care team, which includes lab technicians, nutritionists, and therapists involved in occupational, physical, pulmonary, and speech therapy, among others. The object is to work together to speed the patient's recovery to health, and the R.N. or licensed practical nurse is in a key position to coordinate the activities of all members of the team, including nurses' aides, orderlies, and ward clerks.

From the above breakdown of nursing specialties, both in and out of the hospital, it is clear that nursing has become a highly specialized profession. It is the responsibility of nurses to be up to date on new technology, medications, and treatments. And continuing education is a must in this field. To get some idea of how all of these demands on the nurse's training and experience come together, let's look at several real-life case histories:

Sherry N. is an orthopedic nurse. She works in the office of a physician who specializes in orthopedic surgery. Many of their patients are suffering from strains, sprains, torn ligaments, muscle fractures, and dislocations. Sherry's job is to take the patient's history, to assist the doctor with his treatment plan, and to instruct the patient on how to avoid future injuries and pain.

Sherry works about thirty-six hours a week. "My hours vary somewhat, but they're ordinarily Monday through Friday. I get down to the office about 7:00 A.M. and there's a full schedule of patients to see. The first thing I do is bring the patient to the exam room, take a history, and do a brief screening. I take the patient's blood pressure and ask about the injury or complaint—how long has it been a problem, and what, if anything, he or she has done to correct it.

"When the doctor examines the patient, I take down everything that he says and I take notes for the patient. After the examination, I review with the patient everything the doctor told him or her—the diagnosis, the plan for treatment, and any instructions to do at home. I might give the patient samples of the medication and explain any possible side effects. If ordered, I might administer a cortisone injection or take an x-ray.

"The job involves a lot of patient contact, and that's very satisfactory, because with the exception of some elderly people who have fractured hips or broken bones, I'm dealing with people who are already in good health and are motivated to stay healthy. Besides, the hours are good and I get to work with a lot of different people from various age groups. I also get to use a lot of the knowledge that I learned in nursing school. It's a good chance to apply my education and nursing skills.

"Sure, there's some pressure. People are anxious to get back on their feet and they want to be able to lead normal lives as quickly as possible. But that's true of just about all patients, and something that you expect when dealing with the public. But patients who have undergone hip or knee surgery or who have had fractures repaired need time to heal, and you try to assure them that it's just a matter of time before they are as good as new."

Twenty-eight-year-old Jennifer K. has a bachelor's degree in nursing (B.N.) and has worked part-time in a community health center for several years while studying to get her master's degree in community health nursing. Following completion of her nursing studies, she and another nurse with a master's degree in medical-surgical nursing began a private nursing practice in the community where they live.

On an average day, Jennifer will see a variety of patients—perhaps an elderly woman who wants to discuss how to work with her bedridden husband, or a diabetic middle-aged woman who has questions about diet and administering insulin injections. One night a week she and her partner work with a group of diabetic patients on proper diet and nutrition, low blood sugar levels, and the emotional problems created by the disease.

Thirty-three-year-old Ann, a nurse practitioner in family practice, received her bachelor's degree at a large state university in Ohio. Prior to that she had received a certificate in nursing at a local community college. When her husband was transferred to Chicago, she got a job at a large university-affiliated hospital downtown. But since they lived in the suburbs, the commute downtown and back got to be a problem, so she accepted a job at a family practice clinic closer to home, where for two years she did both family practice and industrial nursing.

Prior to becoming an NP, she had worked as a surgical nurse for several years, primarily in the pulmonary area. It was in surgery that she first noticed nurse practitioners working in the medical-surgical area. The NPs seemed to be able to do everything that she had dreamt of doing in medicine without having to go to medical school. Being a parent, she thought that the NP program offered everything that she wanted, and at a considerably higher salary than what she was making.

After earning her master's degree as a nurse practitioner, she obtained a position in a family practice clinic, working with several other physicians. In her new job, she was the first NP hired in the practice. At first she was apprehensive about how the patients would accept her, but her fears proved groundless; on her first few weeks on the job she saw more than a hundred patients.

As a nurse practitioner she estimates that she can handle about 80 to 90 percent of the cases that present themselves to medical doctors. If she suspects that a patient with a sore throat might have strep throat, she would do a throat culture or a rapid strep test. If the test comes back positive, she would give the patient an antibiotic to stop the infection. Recently, NPs in Illinois were allowed to prescribe many medications with the supervising physician's cosignature.

SALARY AND WORKING CONDITIONS

To give you a better idea of what nursing has to offer, let's take a look at what you would earn as a nurse and under what conditions you would be working.

Earnings

According to the Bureau of Labor Statistics (BLS), median weekly earnings of all full-time nurses were $682 in 2000. This equals total earnings of about $35,464 per year. Annual earnings of the middle 50 percent were between $24,430 and $49,070, according to the BLS. If you were in the lowest 10 percent, your annual earnings would have been less than $29,480 and if you were in the top 10 percent, your annual earnings would have topped $69,300.

Median annual earning in industries employing the largest numbers of R.N.s in 1998 were as follows:

personnel health services	$43,000
hospitals	$39,900
home health care services	$39,200
offices and clinics of M.D.s	$36,500
nursing and personal care facilities	$36,300

For staff R.N.s in chain nursing homes, annual salaries were somewhat lower, averaging $32,200, according to the Buck Survey of the American Health Care Association in 1996. The middle 50 percent earned between $29,000 and $35,400.

According to *Nursing 2001*'s annual survey of subscribers, new R.N.s average $16.24 an hour, while new L.P.N.s earn $11.88 an hour. But the numbers vary quite a bit by location, as the following table shows:

	R.N.	L.P.N./L.V.N.
New England	$17.07	$14.65
Middle Atlantic	$16.78	$12.08
East North Central	$16.30	$12.60
West North Central	$14.70	$10.84
South Atlantic	$15.74	$11.53
East South Central	$14.29	$10.11
West South Central	$15.04	$10.63
Mountain	$15.75	$11.76
Pacific	$18.28	$14.16

In all cases, salaries varied according to geographic area, the kind of service provided, the size of the hospital, and the type of hospital. For example, R.N.s in community hospitals earned $17.50 per hour, those working in private hospitals earned $18.10 per hour, and those working for university-affiliated hospitals earned $18.20 per hour.

Likewise for those working in New England or the Pacific Coast, earnings would be $17.07 and $18.28 respectively per hour, as compared with $14.70 per hour in the Plains states or $14.29 per hour in the mid-South states.

Do advanced degrees help? They most certainly do. *Nursing 2001*'s survey showed that only 10 percent of those with associate degrees earned more than $50,000 a year, while 16 percent of the R.N.s with bachelor's degrees and a whopping 40 percent of R.N.s with master's degrees earned more than $50,000 a year.

Certification was another plus. Here *Nursing 2001*'s survey showed an average annual salary of $46,446 for certified nurses, as opposed to $39,573 for noncertified nurses.

Also affecting salaries was the size of the institution, with the survey revealing that hospital salaries increased along with number of beds. As might be expected, the more experienced the R.N., the more likely the salary would increase.

A final influence on salaries was the nursing shortage, with 32 percent of the survey respondents reporting that their hospitals now offer signing bonuses for new hires.

Working Conditions

On the whole, working conditions for nurses, both R.N.s and L.P.N.s, are excellent. In most cases you work in clean, well-lit, comfortable facilities. In home health care or public health, you would have to travel to patients' homes and to schools, community centers, and other job sites. To withstand the emotional strains of coping with human suffering, emergencies, and patients who may take out their frustrations and depression on you, you must be emotionally stable. And because patients in hospitals and nursing homes require round-the-clock care weekends as well as weekdays, you may have to work weekends, nights, and holidays. You may also have to be on call, which means that for twenty-four hours or more, you will have to be available to serve the needs of patients who may be admitted to the hospital or to supplement the needs of nurses on duty, as required. But if you work in an office, in industrial or occupational health, or in public health, your hours would be more regular.

Nursing, however, has its hazards. In hospitals, nursing homes, and clinics there is always the possibility that you may have to care for persons with AIDS, hepatitis, or other infectious diseases—although there is little risk of infection if you observe proper precautions. And to guard against the risk of radiation, or possible injury from exposure to anesthetics and chemicals used for sterilization of instruments, you must at all times follow hospital procedures. In addition, there is the possibility of injury when moving or lifting patients, shocks from electrical equipment, or hazards stemming from compressed gases.

For more of what nursing has to offer, read on. Chapter 4 talks about the personal qualities it takes to succeed in nursing, how to tell if nursing is right for you, and the pros and cons of working as a nurse.

C H A P T E R

4

CAN YOU MAKE IT IN NURSING?

From what you have read so far, does nursing seem to be the kind of career in which you would be interested and, equally important, is it the kind of career that matches your skills and aptitudes that are so important to success? This chapter will help answer these critical questions.

IMPORTANT CHANGES IN NURSING

In recent years some serious and disturbing issues have affected the profession, and you should consider them very carefully before making the time and financial commitment that is required to go into nursing. Several critical changes in nursing, particularly in hospital or acute care nursing, have thrown the field upside down. Changes in the delivery of health care—specifically downsizing (reducing staff), restructuring (merging into huge health care delivery conglomerates), and the use of unlicensed personnel—have been substantial and far-reaching . . . all in the name of helping to curb runaway health care costs.

A survey of patient care delivery that appeared in the November 1996 issue of the *American Journal of Nursing* contains a lengthy list of findings that were very serious. Taken individually the survey results were serious enough, but taken as a whole they present a disturbing, even shocking, exposé of some major trends. The results, based on more than seven thousand survey participant-respondents, were by far the largest survey of nurse

views on health care ever conducted. Here are a few of the more disquiet-
ing of these findings:

Nurses across the board and in all job settings reported overwhelmingly
that they're taking care of more patients (66 percent) and have been cross-
trained to handle more responsibilities.

What's more, the responses suggest that efforts to increase productivity
through "speedups" (handling more patients in less time) or expecting
fewer workers to do more work are not restricted to nurses at bedside.
Almost half the respondents reported cuts in nurse managers, and almost
two out of five reported losses of nurses at the executive level.

Overall, more than half of the respondents noted that their facilities had
closed beds or units during the past year, with the deepest cuts reported in
the Northeast and mid-Atlantic regions. But more encouragingly, even as
nurses everywhere reported that their facilities were downsizing, an almost
equal number of nurses reported that their hospitals were adding services.

Adding to the news about the shrinking job market for nurses was an
unprecedented number of mergers in 1997, in which hospitals scrambled
to beat competition and increase their bargaining position. Some 445 community hospitals were involved in mergers in 1995, while dozens of others
closed their doors for good. Understandably, nurses are quite concerned
about how all of these changes will affect their jobs.

The survey further found that "it seems clear that job prospects for R.N.s
in hospitals across the country are diminishing . . . employment forecasts
of the Bureau of Labor Statistics predict that by 2005 the percentage of
nurses employed in hospitals will shrink from 60 percent to 57.4 percent."

In recent years, however, the employment situation for R.N.s seems to
have taken a turn for the better. The Bureau of Labor Statistics (BLS) now
foresees a faster-than-average growth for employment of R.N.s as compared with all other occupations through 2008. In addition, the BLS sees a
demand for R.N.s in such fields as home health, long-term care, and ambulatory care.

Even so, nurses can expect longer working hours, more patients to care
for in fewer hours, less job satisfaction, greater concern about job security,
and less pride in their work. And this in turn tends to create more job tension and more likelihood for mistakes, which could affect patient care badly
and might cause more nurse burnout and increased numbers of nurses
leaving the profession, especially in hospital care.

Here are some typical comments gleaned from a thousand randomly selected replies to the American Nurses Association (ANA) survey:

> The new attitude since a recent merger . . . at our facility by a large, business-oriented company is: "Do it and like it or you will be replaced—the nursing market is saturated."
> —*Twenty-six-year-old ICU/CCU staff nurse from Ohio*

> I've especially seen a decrease in patient satisfaction with the emergence of care partners. It's frightening in pediatrics to have so few R.N.s due to increased floating, part-time R.N.s, and cross-trained personnel. It's not safe.
> —*Thirty-one-year-old ICU/CCU pediatrics staff nurse from Alabama*

> There's been an increase in disciplinary actions against nurses in order to (I believe) keep the blame and responsibility from sticking to administration for poor staffing and management.
> —*Forty-seven-year-old staff nurse from California*

Heard enough? Here's just one more comment, as published in the January 1997 issue of the *American Journal of Nursing*:

> Recently you hear more and more horror stories from family, friends, and patients about their hospital stays. I find myself constantly on the defensive, trying to explain why these deficits exist. The fact is that they should not exist. People come to the hospital in crisis. They should feel safe and confident that they'll receive sensitive, skilled care without excuses, but this isn't what's happening.
>
> —*Nurse from Sayville, New York*

But lest you get the idea that all is doom and gloom in nursing, particularly in acute care or hospital work, be assured that this is not the case by any means. True, hospital downsizing, largely in response to managed care, has created greater hardships for smaller nursing staffs, which in many cases are expected to care for ever-increasing numbers of patients.

But the fact remains that of the dozens of nurses interviewed for this book, only a few had anything negative to say about the profession. Most were very satisfied with the job, with the benefits, and particularly with the joy in helping to speed the recovery to health of their patients. Here are a few typical comments:

> If I can help my patients to gain some relief or to relieve some stress reaction, I get my thanks from the patients' smile when they say to me, "I am feeling so much better now. Thanks a million."
>
> —*Ward nurse*

> This job is so exciting, helping patients to feel better, working with and interpreting the patient's charts. I guess what I like best is that I am able to help the patient to recover. For example, by spending some extra time with patients, we are able to get them in a more relaxed frame of mind, and they recover much more quickly.
>
> —*Nurse manager for a surgical intensive care unit*

> I enjoy working with people, and nursing lets me do just that. The challenge and the opportunity to serve are there at all times, and I feel that through my work at this hospital, I could practice in just about any facility in the country, and earn a good salary on top of it.
>
> —*Nurse with a two-year-old child to support*

So there it is. For every adverse reaction to nursing that we could possibly cite, double or triple that number have made their careers in nursing and are enjoying every minute of it.

WHAT DOES IT TAKE TO SUCCEED?

What qualities do you need to succeed in nursing? A recent survey in the *American Journal of Nursing* lists several. Let's look at each in depth.

Emotional Frame of Mind or Temperament

How well you fare under various circumstances and situations will depend largely on your temperament. For instance, it takes coolness and ability to work under stress to work in the operating room, where your action must be quick and sure when the surgeon requests a particular piece of equipment or some other response of you. Working in medical-surgical or pediatrics is a little less stressful and might be better suited to you if you prefer a slower and less anxious atmosphere. Here are some questions that you should ask yourself:

• Do I feel excited or challenged when I have several projects going at once? (Emergency department nursing might be right for you.)

• Am I easily bored by routine? (Again, you might consider going into emergency room nursing, or nursing in intensive care or surgery.)

• Do I enjoy helping to solve frustrating problems that appear insoluble? (Such problems might include getting the dose right for a patient who requires a special cholesterol medication that may be good for his or her cholesterol but may tend to make the patient irritable and highly nervous.)

Physical Endurance

Obviously you should be in good shape and have plenty of stamina to withstand the physical demands of nursing. You will be on your feet a good portion of the time, and you have to cover long distances in the course of your work, from the patient bedside to the pharmacy, to physical therapy, and so on.

People Skills

Nursing requires that you should be comfortable working with patients—patients of every kind—some mean, nasty, and overbearing and others as pleasant as can be. This is particularly important in most nursing environments, where your contact with patients is firsthand and immediate. However, in the area of intensive care, you may be more concerned with the patient's physical condition as seen on a monitor. Here are a few questions to ask yourself:

• Am I more comfortable observing how patients are doing, or do I prefer hands-on contact with patients?

• Am I good in comforting patients when they get upset for whatever reason, even for reasons that may seem silly or immature?

- Am I a good listener?
- Am I more comfortable treating and caring for certain age groups or working in certain settings? (If, for instance, you are more comfortable working in areas with an accent on challenge or drama, then intensive care might be the place for you. If you are more oriented toward a personal approach with your patients, you might consider a medical-surgical or children's unit.)

Manual Dexterity

It takes a good deal of manual dexterity to do a wide variety of nursing tasks, such as administering shots, setting up for intravenous medication or feeding of patients, drawing blood samples, changing a dressing on a wound, and injecting a catheter—to name but a few. Obviously you must have good coordination of your fingers and hands to accomplish these tasks. In this area, here are some questions to ask yourself:

- Do I get nervous or flustered when assigned unexpected or complex treatments to handle?
- Am I comfortable working with new equipment and the latest in medical technology?

Leadership Ability

Some roles in hospital nursing call for leadership ability. For example, working with patients recuperating from surgery or from an infectious disease might call for immediate action from you, in the event the patient takes a turn for the worse and there is no one else available. Can you handle this kind of pressure? Or would you rather have someone else present to turn to? Ask yourself:

- Do I enjoy working alone (as in private or home nursing) or with groups (as in most bedside hospital nursing)?

Mental or Problem-Solving Skills

Sometimes referred to as cognitive skills, this simply measures your ability to think through a problem, analyze it, and determine the best course of action to solve it. If you enjoy challenge, you will prefer new and unexpected situations, as in emergency or operating room nursing, and you will constantly strive to update your skills. Ask yourself:

- Do I tend to welcome situations where I have to rely primarily on myself, or do I need the support of others?
- Do I prefer to learn a few things well, or would I rather learn a lot of things quickly?
- Is taking on new situations and challenges a part of my makeup, or does it make me nervous?

Above all, you must have a true dedication to helping others and a love for helping people in need. As already noted, patients who are ill can often be mean and crotchety, and they can vent their frustration and pain on you. Without a genuine love of people, it is doubtful that you can take this kind of stress.

You must have more than your share of patience and tact. Patients who are ill can be very demanding and expect instant satisfaction to their problems or complaints. Since you are dealing with many patients, it may be impossible to provide instant gratification to a given patient's needs. Explaining this can require a lot of patience and diplomacy.

Also, in your work with patients, you are often privy to certain personal parts of their lives, which calls for tact and complete trust. Thus, if a patient tells you something in confidence, you cannot relay this information indiscriminately. Confidential information can only be told to another health care official if it is relevant to working out a treatment plan for the patient.

Other Skills

In addition to these, the American Nurses Association lists several other skills as being critical for anyone considering a career in nursing:

Effective, Clear Communications Skills

Nurses must be able to clearly communicate to patients as well as to administrators, associates, and subordinates. They should be able to articulate what it takes to meet the hospital's need for efficiency as well as the nurse's own obligation to deliver high quality and competent care, and to convince patients of the need to follow instructions in helping them regain good health.

Awareness of Nursing Legislation and Policy

Nurses should strive to keep up with laws and regulations that affect the quality of health care delivery, and they should be aware of current trends and policy changes that can affect their ability to deliver quality care.

Leadership Skills

It is not enough for R.N.s to help other members of the health care team to cope with changes in the system. They should also anticipate what is required in the setting of patient care goals and needs.

Organizational and Time Management Strategies

With heavier workloads and shrinking resources, it is more important than ever that R.N.s learn how to manage their time and organize their jobs in view of shifting assignments, and that they are able to establish priorities for assignments.

IS NURSING RIGHT FOR YOU?

We have just enumerated some of the qualifications, personal and emotional, that you need in order to succeed in nursing. How do you know if you are right for nursing if you have not had any personal experience in caring for patients or exposure to patients in a hospital environment? The answer is to get involved, right now, while you are in school.

There are many things that you can do in school to help give you a running start in your chosen profession. For one, begin to write to various nursing schools, public and private, to find out what their admissions policies are, their procedures, and what courses are required. This will help to ensure that you have the required courses and subject majors that you will need to get into nursing school. And these can vary from school to school, so write to several. One school, for instance, may require a B average in high school, another a B-, and so forth.

Next take all the biology, chemistry, behavioral science (psychology and sociology), math, humanities, and literature classes that you can, since you will have to have these subjects out of the way before you can be accepted in nursing school.

Then try to talk to as many nurses as you can about the work, the qualifications, what a typical day is like, and so forth. The more nurses you talk to, the better, since there are so many different types of nursing to explore.

If you can, try to get part-time work in a hospital—after school or on weekends or in the evening. You may be able to get a job as an orderly, helping to transport patients around the hospital, or as a nurse's aide. Even if jobs are not so readily available, hospitals are always on the lookout for volunteers—high-school candy stripers and the like. Here you might be assigned to deliver mail, transport patients around the hospital, and handle various other assignments. The object is to become familiar with working in a hospital or health care environment to see what nurses do and how they react under various conditions.

Also, check with your guidance counselor to see what career materials he or she might have on hand—booklets, videotapes, and so forth. Write to some of the nursing organizations listed at the end of this book. Many of them publish booklets on what is involved in working in specific areas of nursing, such as orthopedics, ophthalmology, and pediatrics. Learn as much as you can about the field before you make the considerable investment in time, finances, and effort that is involved in qualifying for a nursing career. Try to make sure that nursing offers you the kinds of challenges and rewards that you are looking for and for which you are suited.

One final comment: the National League for Nursing has established a career center known as the NLN Center for Career Advancement, which may help to match your needs and skills to opportunities in nursing. Upon request, it will send you reliable information on nursing programs through its network. It can even do a computerized search that will match your needs and talents to specific programs through use of its database. The center offers exclusive career information aimed at shaping your career decision. Call the NLN Center for Career Advancement at (800) 669-9656, ext. 160, for a brochure or for information.

Once you have decided on a nursing career, you are ready for the next step—to see what is involved in gaining admittance to a nursing school and succeeding while there. We will discuss this in the next chapter.

CHAPTER

5

GETTING INTO THE RIGHT NURSING SCHOOL

There are several routes that lead to accreditation as an R.N. and eligibility for the state boards required to practice nursing in all states. Whatever the route you choose, your first step will be to apply to nursing school.

APPLYING TO NURSING SCHOOL

What is involved in applying to a nursing school? Perhaps the first point to consider is whether the school is accredited. Usually, if a school is accredited it means that it has been approved for nursing training by the state in which it is located or by the National League for Nursing. Each state awards schools of nursing approval to operate through standards developed by the state board of nurse examiners.

Even more exhaustive, perhaps, are the standards for accreditation of the National League for Nursing. Such accreditation, which is strictly voluntary, is used in reviewing programs that have been developed to prepare practical and registered nurses in associate's degree, hospital, and bachelor's and master's degree programs.

Standards that have been developed by experts review areas such as curriculum and how the faculty implements it, and faculty preparation. Although such accreditation by the NLN is not compulsory, most nursing programs have sought such approval and received accreditation. At present, many programs awarding master's or doctorate degrees require graduation from an NLN-approved undergraduate program for admission. And, in addition, several state and federal financial assistance programs offer funds only to NLN-accredited schools.

Once you have decided which schools you wish to apply to, it's a good idea to begin the application process as soon as possible—preferably during your junior year in high school. Check the school catalog or other admissions requirements to make sure that you have the required subjects and grades. Each school has its own requirements, so it's essential to write to each to find out which courses are required—such as chemistry, science, and biology—and the number of credits required in each subject or area, as well as the minimum grade point average and other requirements. You will probably have to supply several letters of recommendation from your teachers, and you may be required to write a brief essay as to why you believe study at the particular institution will benefit you. Also, you may have to come in for a personal interview. If you are applying to several schools, it would pay to try to group the interviews together as much as possible. For example, try to group interviews with schools on the West Coast close together; this will minimize travel between schools and unnecessary trips back and forth to visit different schools.

Even if a personal interview is not required, it is a good idea to visit the school so you can check out the facilities for yourself and get a better idea of the training program. If you do visit the school, try to talk to some students to see what they have to say—what they like or dislike about it. Also, try to talk to the financial officer about financial assistance available, loans, scholarships, work-study programs, and other assistance. For a very useful, all-in-one guide to applying to nursing schools, read *How to Get into the Right Nursing Program*, by Carla S. Rogers, Ph.D. (VGM Career Books).

MAJOR NURSING PROGRAMS

Originally, nurses received almost no classroom preparation. Instead, training was hospital-based in an apprenticeship system, in which older students taught younger ones how to take care of patients. This way students provided cheap labor for hospitals. Today, however, the training situation is much different. Let's now take a look at the major nursing programs to see what each involves and how they compare.

Programs for Licensed Practical Nurses

Licensed practical nurses, or L.P.N.s, receive an education and license very different from that of R.N.s. The program lasts approximately a year and includes both classroom work and training in a hospital. Programs are offered primarily through vocational and technical schools, and graduates must pass a state licensing examination, known as the NCLEX–PN, before they can practice. (It should be noted that this is not the same test that is taken by R.N.s.) After passing the examination, the graduates can use the initials L.P.N. after their names and practice under the supervision of a registered nurse. There were more than a thousand training programs for L.P.N.s in 1998, a drop over previous years. Licensed practical nurses today number about seven hundred thousand.

If you are thinking of becoming a nurse but do not want to take the courses, particularly science courses, involved in a degree program, you might find the L.P.N. program best suited for you. It is far less costly than are the programs for R.N.s.

Hospital-School Diploma Programs

Forty years ago nearly all the nurses working in hospitals were graduates of hospital nursing programs. They often ended up working in the hospitals where they trained—the so-called diploma schools—which offered three years of post–high school training leading to the R.N. designation. Hospital-based, or diploma programs, provided a sound educational background for nursing programs that offered both theoretical learning and practical experience. The aim of diploma training was to prepare nurses for giving bedside care in hospitals, nursing homes, other institutions, and in patients' homes.

Today, the diploma, or three-year hospital schools, are still in existence, but they have been very much on the decline. From a high point of more than one thousand hospital-based diploma schools for nurses in 1909, the diploma program has declined to the point where it is currently being offered in only 119 hospitals, and these hospital programs are rapidly being phased out.

Most of the few remaining diploma programs still offered by hospitals are now affiliated with a college in which nursing students can take courses in academic subjects as well as practical courses in nursing. In recent years, however, a few hospitals have applied to state boards of higher education for the right to award an associate's degree in nursing.

Graduates of such programs can take the licensing examination of the state in which they wish to practice. Upon passing they are eligible to practice nursing and to use the initials R.N. (registered nurse) after their names.

Graduates usually assume staff positions in hospitals, often the hospitals where they train, but not necessarily so. Advancement beyond staff nurse is unlikely without additional training.

Associate's Degree Program

The associate's degree program has come on strong since being introduced in the United States in 1952. This program, which was intended to make it easier for many would-be nurses to access the profession when originally introduced, is a two-year program offered primarily in about eleven hundred community or junior colleges and in a few four-year colleges, in settings usually away from hospital schools. Associate's degree programs strongly emphasize technical skills supported by a basic foundation in biological and behavioral sciences. Besides being a shorter program, the associate's degree program is also less expensive than the four-year or bachelor's degree program. Graduates of such programs can find work in hospitals or nursing homes, but usually they do not have the career advancement opportunities open to graduates of bachelor's degree programs.

Admission requirements for such programs range from open policies in a city or community system to fairly strict requirements for private schools. In most cases you must be a high school graduate and have a good scholastic record.

The course of study is about equally divided between nursing skill, or technical, courses and general education courses. Also, if you are taking courses in math or science, you will attend the same classes as students who are not nursing majors, which can be a good thing as it provides a chance for exchange of ideas between nursing students and other students.

A typical program might stress attendance at a nursing clinical laboratory twice weekly for eight hours, two hours of nursing theory for four hours a week, and three to six hours of other college courses every week. Courses are also offered on a part-time or evening basis.

In the laboratory, you have a place to test out nursing theories taught in the classroom in a real hospital situation involving real patients. At the same time, you would use the college laboratory to learn nursing skills such as taking blood pressure, learning how to use an IV (intravenous device) for drugs or nutrition, and testing out bandaging techniques.

Ordinarily, the associate's degree program gives you more options than hospital-prepared nurses have. But it's important to realize that if you want to study for a bachelor's or master's degree program, some of your credits may not apply, and you may be required to take additional courses to qualify.

On the other hand, completion of the associate's degree program may qualify you for admission to several nursing schools that award the bachelor's degree in only two years. In other words, the credits you receive studying for your associate's degree are the equivalent of two years of a four-year program, and you only need to complete two years of additional study to receive the bachelor's degree.

Currently, there are 876 such programs listed by the National League for Nursing, accounting for by far the largest number of nursing programs and the largest group of graduating nurses. The American Nurses Association estimates that about 28 percent of the nurses practicing today are graduates of associate's degree programs, as compared to 30 percent who are graduates of four-year bachelor's degree programs. But while this is the least expensive program for nurses, it is anticipated that R.N.s with more advanced educational backgrounds will have the best chances for finding employment in hospitals and other health care facilities.

Nursing graduates of associate's degree programs are also qualified to take the state licensing examination and can practice nursing and use the initials R.N.

Of the R.N.s practicing today, who are estimated to be more than 2.1 million, by far the largest percentage are graduates of associate's degree programs. However, an ever-growing number of R.N.s are receiving their training in bachelor's degree programs. Associate's degree programs can get you started in a hospital or office as a staff nurse; but to advance to any position of authority in a hospital or in research or teaching, you will need at the very least the bachelor's degree, and, in some cases, a master's degree or Ph.D.

Degree Programs

Often referred to as a baccalaureate program, the four-year program is offered in 520 colleges and universities throughout the United States. In the bachelor's program, courses are a combination of general liberal arts courses in languages and the humanities or literature, as well as the full scope of nursing theory and science, with specialized professional nursing classes and clinical laboratory experience working with hospital or institutionalized patients. It also provides the foundation for more advanced work should you decide to go on and study for a master's or Ph.D. degree. It is essential that you learn what courses are required for entrance into such programs. Most often you will have to have some liberal arts, biology, chemistry (two semesters), anatomy and physiology, English, and physics.

In the four-year program, in the junior and senior years you concentrate on nursing theory and practice, while the first two years focus on liberal arts and basic science courses—biology, chemistry, anatomy, microbiology, physiology, and a few other science and psychology courses. In many cases you can attend a junior college or university for the first two years and transfer to a nursing program for the final two years of training. As is true of associate's degree programs, you are held to the same standards of performance as are students in non-nursing courses.

Nursing courses and many of the science courses include a laboratory session. A typical program might look something like this: an 8:00 A.M. to 1:00 P.M. clinical lab in a hospital or nursing home, four mornings a week; a 4:00 to 6:00 P.M. psychology class; and a 6:00 to 8:00 P.M. nursing theory class. The fifth day might feature a nursing rotation, in which you receive exposure to some particular kind of nursing: geriatrics (elderly patients), pediatrics (young children), emergency medicine, or any of a dozen other nursing specialties.

Some schools feature what is known as the *generic* or *integrated* program, which integrates nursing courses with those in the liberal arts and sciences, starting in either the freshman year or the first semester of the sophomore year.

After completing a bachelor's degree, you must pass the National Council Licensure Examination for Registered Nurses (NCLEX–RN) to obtain a license to practice nursing and to use the R.N. title. State boards of nursing decide licensing requirements, set continuing education and competency standards, and handle any disciplinary actions against R.N.s.

Completion of a four-year or bachelor's degree program enables you not only to provide professional nursing care to patients and their families, but also to assume lower-level leadership positions as a health care coordinator. And you can work in various health care settings, including health promotion programs, HMOs, well-baby clinics, hospitals, and nursing homes. By training and orientation, the bachelor's program trains you to seek out solutions to situations that are unusual and to supervise the care provided by subordinate team members.

There are several options available to college graduates. For example, if you have a bachelor's degree, certain nursing schools offer a four-semester nursing program that upon completion will award you with a master's degree.

R.N.s who have completed either associate's degree or diploma programs may, through articulation, be awarded the bachelor's degree following two years of nursing study. But note that if you are involved in a program that leads to a Bachelor of Science in health education, health administration, or occupational health, these degrees may not be considered the equivalent of a B.S. in nursing. Consequently, they may not be acceptable for advanced nursing education such as a master's program or the nurse practitioner or nurse anesthesiologist programs. In this case, you might be required to take certain other courses that would not be required in the B.S. in nursing program.

Advanced training is required for several advanced practice nursing positions. These are:

1. **Nurse Practitioner.** Most of the 150 education programs in the United States confer a master's degree. In at least thirty-six states you must be certified by the ANA or a specialty nursing organization.

2. **Clinical Nurse-Midwife.** This position requires an average of about a year and a half of specialized post–nursing school training, either in an accredited certificate program or, like nurse practitioners, at the master's level.

3. **Clinical Nurse Specialist.** These nurse specialists have advanced degrees—master's or doctoral—that qualify them to practice in any of several specialized areas of clinical practice, such as mental health, gerontology, cardiac or cancer care, and community or neonatal health.

4. **Certified Registered Nurse Anesthetist.** This position requires two to three years of training beyond the required four-year bachelor's degree, as well as meeting national certification and recertification requirements.

Higher Degree Programs

Master's and doctoral degree programs in nursing almost always require students to be graduates of an accredited four-year program. Emphasis is primarily on research, advanced clinical work, and training for applicants who wish to work as teachers and administrators.

ARTICULATION

Articulation is the means by which you can advance to a higher level of nursing. For example, there are any number of schools that offer articulation programs for L.P.N.s who may want to become registered nurses, or for nurses who want to go from a diploma to an associate's, bachelor's, or master's degree program. You might begin your nursing career with a diploma or associate's degree (two-year) and decide you want to get a bachelor's or master's degree in nursing. There are many schools that offer such articulation—you might think of them as advancement in education—to qualified graduates of lower-level nursing programs, and they are listed in the *National League for Nursing Guide to Undergraduate Education*. This handy book contains information on all accredited diploma, associate's, and baccalaureate (four-year) programs, including enrollment, affiliation (public or private), and whom to contact.

So that leaves the question of which route to follow to get your R.N.—diploma, associate's, or bachelor's degree. To decide, ask yourself the following questions:

- What are my financial resources?
- What are my academic capabilities?
- What are my long-term goals as a nurse?

If, for instance, you have limited funds and are only a fair student, you might consider pursuing training leading to an L.P.N. degree, which will entitle you to assume many staff posts in hospitals and nursing homes at a slightly lower level than that of an R.N. The pay is good, estimated at about $24,700 per year in 2000 for new L.P.N.s, and opportunities are improving as many hospitals downsize and assign more duties to L.P.N.s working under the supervision of an R.N.

Similarly, if you are limited in funds but a good student, you might consider a diploma program, which is less expensive than an associate's or bachelor's program, still leads to the R.N. designation, and will enable you to practice as an R.N. once you pass the state boards. But, as has already been noted, these programs are rapidly being phased out and only about a hundred are left.

The associate's degree will allow you to handle any professional nursing job in any setting—hospital, nursing home, clinic, or emergency room facility—but you may have to have additional training to qualify for supervisory, teaching, or research posts.

Like the associate's degree, the bachelor's degree will qualify you for any professional-level nursing program. Increasingly, the bachelor's degree in nursing (B.S.N.) is a requirement for graduate study in research, consulting, teaching, or clinical specialization. Indeed, some career paths are open only to nurses who have a bachelor's or advanced degree (advanced nursing, for instance, usually requires a master's degree to qualify).

You should also be aware that there has been discussion of raising the educational requirements of an R.N. to a bachelor's degree, but so far this is just talk. If and when such changes become law, on a state by state basis, they would not affect R.N. graduates of diploma or associate's degree programs, who would be "grandfathered in." This simply means that they could still practice as R.N.s, even though they do not have the bachelor's degree. Still, with the demand for skilled nurses rapidly increasing, it seems certain that nurses with better educational credentials will have a much better chance of getting a job.

PAYING FOR NURSING SCHOOL

Although some funds for nursing programs have been shrinking, federal and state resources are still there as well as public resources, including federal and state scholarships, loans, and work-study programs. Nearly all schools and universities have their own private scholarship and loan funds available to students who have good scholastic records and who can demonstrate need. Also many community groups, such as local Lions or Kiwanis Clubs, may offer scholastic or loan aid to children of members or to students from their respective communities.

Most financial aid to pay for your nursing education comes through the school itself, regardless of whether it involves federal, state, or private sources, or the school's own funds. The funds are based on proven need for assistance, not just on merit. It is important to start investigating what schools have to offer in financial aid as soon as you begin shopping around for a nursing school. Remember, too, that most schools take into consideration parental financial information when creating an aid package.

Also remember that even though a nursing education at a state or publicly supported school is usually a fraction of what a private school might cost, the financial aid package available from the private school might be considerably higher than what you could expect to receive from the public school. Further, you should realize that to qualify for the low tuition of a public school you must be a state resident, as tuition for out-of-state students is considerably higher.

Costs of tuition and living expenses for students studying nursing at the associate's degree level are about the same as what they would be for other students enrolled in the junior or community college. If you live in the community in which the college is located, your tuition will be considerably less than if you lived elsewhere in the state, since local residents do enjoy a considerable tuition reduction by law.

Once you are accepted by a school, it will figure out a financial package for you based on federal and state loan sources available to the school, its own private loan and scholarship resources, and scholarships and grants available from various private philanthropic organizations and individuals.

Admission by a school does not commit you to attend. You can decide after comparing the financial package that the school offers as well as its educational program and facilities.

According to the College Board, loans are a very basic part of any financial aid package, accounting for nearly half of all financial assistance awarded to students. Many excellent loan funds are available, including the Perkins Loan—formerly known as the National Direct Student Loan—which charges only 5 percent interest not payable until nine months after you finish school.

With that in mind, let's look at a few of these sources of financial aid.

Federal Aid Programs

Since all of the funds listed here depend upon congressional appropriations on a year-by-year basis, you cannot necessarily count on having this money available in years to come. But they were available as of 2001–02. It should be noted that NLN-approved programs are eligible to take part in all federal aid programs. To check on eligibility of other nursing programs, check with their financial aid offices.

The Pell Grant

This is the primary source of undergraduate support for most college students, including nursing school students. Grants, which currently range up to $4,000 a year, depend on your financial need, cost of tuition, fees, and other factors. The amount you receive under the Pell Grant is then figured into your financial aid package in any participating school. To qualify you must first complete the need analysis form. These grants, you will be happy to know, need not be repaid. You should apply for Pell Grants as soon as possible after January 1, and the deadline for submission of applications is May 1 for the fall semester. For further information request a free copy of the booklet *The Student Guide: Financial Aid from the U.S. Department of Education 2002–2003*. Write to: Federal Student Aid Information Center, P.O. Box 84, Washington, D.C. 20044. The telephone number to call for information is: (800) 4-FED AID.

Supplemental Educational Opportunity Grants (SEOG)

To qualify you must be enrolled at least half-time in an eligible undergraduate program at a school participating in the SEOG program. Only students with exceptional financial need are eligible for these grants, which award as much as $4,000 a year for basic nursing study and require no payback. Participating schools have a limited amount of funds to award students with demonstrated need; the school determines the amount.

College Work-Study Program

This federally supported program provides funds for part-time employment, on or off campus, in participating colleges and universities. The school furnishes jobs at a salary at least equal to the current minimum wage. The school also determines the number of hours to be worked. The financial aid office grants awards based on need. To qualify you must submit completed applications to the nursing schools you are applying to early in the calendar year.

Nursing Student Loan Program, U.S. Department of Health and Human Services

Aimed especially at nursing students, this program makes loans of up to $2,500 per year available for freshman and sophomore students and up to $4,000 per year for juniors and seniors. Awards, based on demonstrated financial need, are available for both undergraduate and graduate nursing study. The aggregate maximum is $13,000 for both undergraduate and graduate borrowing. Repayment of these low-income loans begins nine months after graduation. You are allowed up to ten years to repay the loan, which carries 5 percent interest. Apply to the financial aid offices of the schools of your choice.

Perkins Loans (Formerly National Direct Student Loans)

Participating schools are agents in awarding these federally sponsored loan funds. To qualify you must show financial need and attend nursing school at least half-time. You can borrow up to $6,000 per year to an aggregate maximum of $40,000 total for both undergraduate and graduate studies. Repayment begins nine months after graduation at 5 percent interest. You have up to ten years to repay the loan, which can be deferred under certain conditions.

Stafford Loans (formerly Guaranteed Student Loans), PLUS Loans, SLS Loans

This program, guaranteed by state guarantee agencies or the federal government, makes loans available at a maximum interest rate of 8.25 percent to students who are new borrowers. You must arrange these loans privately through banks, credit unions, savings and loan associations, and so forth. Under this loan program, you can borrow as much as $2,625 a year during the first and second years and up to $3,500 to $5,500 a year after that, with a total loan limit of $23,000 for all four years of study. For graduate study, you can borrow up to $8,500 a year or a total of $65,000, which includes all loans for undergraduate and graduate study.

Repayment begins six months after graduation, and the repayment period is quite liberal and may even be deferred or canceled under certain circumstances. The 1 percent loan origination charges are deducted from the amount received. Under the PLUS (for parents of dependent children) program and SLS (for independent students) you can borrow up to $4,000 a year for a total of $23,000 at a 3 percent interest rate. No loan origination fee is charged, nor are these loans based on need. However, you may have to go through a credit investigation to qualify.

Federal Stafford Unsubsidized Loans

If you are a graduate or independent undergraduate student, you are eligible for loans of up to $4,000 a year to a maximum of $20,000 as an undergraduate student and up to $138,500 as a graduate student. Need is not a factor, but the total amount borrowed cannot exceed the cost of education minus all other aid received. The interest rate is tied to the rate of a fifty-two-week Treasury bill plus 3.25 percent, not to exceed 8.25 percent. Interest rates payable quarterly begin while you are still in school, and repayment of principal begins when you are no longer studying full-time.

State Sources of Financial Aid

All states offer grants for education, including nursing study, and a few states even allow for study outside the state. Most of these grants are based on need, and your financial aid office will figure such grants into the total financial package to be awarded.

In addition to these loans and grants, the National League for Nursing's booklet *Scholarships and Loans for Nursing Education: 2001–2002* lists dozens of scholarships and loans specifically earmarked for nursing students, each with its own requirements and places to contact for applications or further information. For information on obtaining this very handy booklet, write to: National League for Nursing, 350 Hudson Street, New York, New York 10014.

The booklet also lists other sources of information on financial aid, some aimed particularly at minority students, such as *Don't Miss Out* by Robert and Anna Leader, Octameron Associates, Inc., P.O. Box 2748, Alexandria, Virginia 22301, which explains how to calculate costs of a nursing school education and discusses alternate routes you can explore to find assistance.

CHOOSING A NURSING SPECIALTY

As we have seen, nursing is a highly specialized field and is becoming increasingly more so every year. How do you know which area of nursing you will want to specialize in? The answer: it is not easy. You may have a pretty good idea of which way you want to go in nursing even before you enter nursing school; but for most, this is a difficult decision.

For most students the choice is made in their junior and senior years, when they are exposed to various nursing specialties during nursing rotations. For instance, you might do ten weeks in a medical-surgical unit during your junior year, in which you would be exposed to various types of medical and surgical patients, including pediatrics, operating room, intensive care, outpatient surgery, and emergency. This might be followed by ten weeks in obstetrics-gynecology, including the neonatal intensive care unit (for critically ill newborns), the labor and delivery rooms, and so forth.

CERTIFICATION

You might be interested in knowing that the January 2001 issue of the *American Journal of Nursing* contains the "Guide to Certification," which lists thirty-five nursing specialties, each with its own requirements for certification and its own certifying board (reprinted in this book; see Appendix D). For example, if you wish to be certified in adult critical care nursing, you must have at least 1,750 hours within the past two years preceding application with 875 hours of experience in the year prior to application. Apply to: AACN Certification Corporation, 101 Columbia, Aliso Viejo, California 92656.

To be certified as a school nurse, on the other hand, you must be a licensed R.N. with a bachelor's degree. In addition, three years' experience is recommended. Urology nurses must have a year's experience in urology. There are fees that must accompany your application and these can range from a few dollars to several hundred dollars.

Is certification important? Absolutely. Specific fields of practice, such as advanced practice nursing, require certification before you can practice. In other specialties it is not required, but it is highly recommended. As a certified emergency or critical care nurse, you can command a higher salary and certain institutions will require that you be certified in your specialty before they will employ you.

CHAPTER

6

GETTING STARTED AND ADVANCING

When the time comes to choose a nursing profession, be sure to take your own preferences into account. For example, do you want to work in an area where there is a lot of action—such as critical care, emergency room, or operating room? Or would you prefer working in areas where the action is not as hectic, but where you might be able to form closer attachments to your patients—such as pediatrics, obstetrics, or surgery?

Then, too, think about pay. Critical care and operating room nurses earn more than general staff nurses in a hospital, but the requirements are greater and so is the pressure. And there is also the factor of where the jobs are located. Currently the majority of the jobs are in hospital care. However, as we will see in Chapter 7, the hospital job market has had its ups and downs, and there will be many more opportunities in community health nursing and in private care nursing, especially since more patients are living longer lives and will need nursing care in their homes.

WHERE ARE THE NURSING JOBS?

According to the Bureau of Health Professions' National Sample Survey of Registered Nurses, of the 2,115,815 people employed in nursing in 2000, the employment setting was as follows:

- 59.1 percent of all nurses were working in hospital settings.
- 18.3 percent worked in a community or public health setting.
- 9.5 percent worked in ambulatory care settings, including nurse solo or group practices and health maintenance organizations.
- 6.9 percent worked in nursing homes or other extended care facilities.
- 2.1 percent worked in settings such as nursing education (schools and universities).
- 3.6 percent worked in national or state administrative offices or associations and in insurance companies and other areas.

HOW TO FIND A JOB

Initially, many nurses obtain jobs in hospitals where they have had their clinical training, where they know the facilities and the nursing personnel, and where the supervisory hospital personnel know them.

However, if you want to work away from the state in which you are licensed, you will first have to determine if the state in which you are looking for employment has reciprocal agreements with the state where you are currently employed. Information regarding fees, eligibility, and forms required for the state nursing boards or exams can be obtained by writing to the state board of nursing; also check Appendix E.

After licensure is ascertained, where do you look for jobs? Probably your first line of inquiry is to contact friends, colleagues, or your school counselor about jobs in your area of interest or agencies that might be able to assist in your job search. Then proceed to contact agencies, health care facilities, or persons who might have been recommended either by a phone call or through a personal visit. An appointment is always advisable and a matter of courtesy. A follow-up phone call or letter advising of your interest in a given position quite often bears fruit. If the person or agency you are contacting has no openings at that time, they may hear of an opening later that they can then refer to you.

Before networking, you might want to contact your own school placement service. Just about all community and four-year nursing schools have such placement offices that help student graduates find jobs. Quite often they will send you bulletins of opportunities in your field that you may wish to follow up on, and they will keep your résumé on file and send it out if your background seems to match up with a prospective employer's needs. Your state nursing association (see Appendix C) also has a job placement service. You might want to contact it for any openings that would match your qualifications and preferences.

Other sources of jobs include nursing opportunities advertised in the classified section of your local newspaper (especially the Sunday edition) and in national and local nursing journals. In addition, there are many employment agencies that specialize in placement of nurses and other health care personnel. Finally, there is your state employment office, which often has job openings that seem to offer possibilities.

Now a word about registry nurses. Each state maintains a list of licensed nurses who are qualified to care for individuals, and the professional registry refers requests for nursing care to nurses whom it considers to have the background and qualifications required. There are commercial registries that help fill shortages in the hospital's regular staff during vacation periods or when a nurse leaves and a qualified replacement has not been found. Such registries vary in the quality of their nurses and the standards that they have set for sending out nurses. It pays, therefore, to get a line on such registries by checking with various referrals or hospital staffs that use nursing registries. Ordinarily, if you are referred to a hospital to fill a temporary staff position, you will be paid at a higher rate than the hospital's own staff nurses. But when you figure that as a registry nurse you receive no employment benefits—paid holidays, vacations, sick pay, pension programs, and so forth—you will actually be getting less than the staff nurse. Still, working as a registry nurse does have its advantages: you are free to work the hours that you prefer and to cite a preference for a given type of nursing.

There is one thing further to comment on in discussing employment as a nurse. Perhaps one of its primary benefits is that if things do not work out as a nurse in a particular section of the hospital, there is always the possibility that you can transfer to another area that may be much more to your liking. Then, too, many nurses—an estimated 25 percent—work part-time, and this is a big consideration if you are raising children and have to be home at a certain hour.

RÉSUMÉ

In seeking employment, one thing that you will need, besides your professional skills and licensure, is a résumé. The résumé, which should not be longer than a page or two, summarizes your professional experience, qualifications, and educational background.

A résumé can serve as a first introduction to a prospective employer. But more often, it is given to a prospective employer after you have had an interview. It serves as a reminder of your qualifications and background and can always be reviewed if and when an opening should occur that would match your qualifications.

In addition to standard data such as name, phone number, and address, a typical résumé also includes the names and addresses of schools attended as well as the degrees earned, major areas of study, and dates attended. Schools should be listed in reverse chronological order—last attended first. List any courses taken that might be particularly relevant to the job in question. This is followed by your employment background, starting with your most recent position and then proceeding backward in order of work experience. Include name and address for each place of employment, dates of employment, job title or titles, and a brief summary of your responsibilities.

Next list any memberships you may hold in professional nursing associations, including any offices held. A list of states in which you are licensed to practice should follow. Don't forget to include any participation you have had in community organizations such as the Girl Scouts, League of Women Voters, and so forth. Include any leadership positions you may have held in these organizations.

The sample résumé that follows is just one of several variations, but it is typical in that it shows what employers are looking for. The object of answering ads, calling friends and relatives for names of prospective employers, updating your résumé, posting it to various Internet websites, and so forth is to get a job—right? But jobs do not just drop out of the sky. Ordinarily, you must first have an interview, and perhaps you will come back for one or more follow-up interviews if the job is a particularly important and responsible one.

Jennifer A. Bryant
885 Circle Drive
Skokie, IL 60076
(847) 555-8234

Objective:

Staff nurse, responsible for recruitment and training of new nurses

Education:

Triton Community College, River Grove, IL

B.S. in Nursing, May 1996

Majored in advanced nursing—150 hours of clinical experience divided among psychiatry, community health services, and neurology

Experience:

- St. Anthony Hospital, Chicago, IL, Staff Nurse
  As an L.P.N., I provided care for 8 to 10 patients on a general postsurgery unit.
- St. Francis Hospital, Blue Island, IL, Candy Striper/Volunteer
  I handled such services as mail delivery and reading to physically disabled patients and children in the pediatric ward. Received the Outstanding Teen Volunteer award for 250 hours of service.

Certification:

Licensed as registered nurse, Illinois, license number 12345

Awards and Honors:

Distinguished Student Award, Triton Community College, 1993
Dean's List, Triton Community College
Student Government Association
President, Student Nurses' Association

INTERVIEW

There are a few things to keep in mind before you go on an interview. First, be punctual. There really is no excuse for being late. Plan on arriving about half an hour early. That way you can allow a little time in case the train is running late or you have trouble finding a place to park, and so on. It is much better to be early than to be late.

Second, dress conservatively. Ordinarily a neat-looking gray or beige suit is appropriate. The interview is not the time to demonstrate your fashion awareness or clothes consciousness. The interviewer's attention should be focused not on how you look but on what you have to say about your qualifications and how you answer his or her questions.

Sometimes interviewers might ask a question that seemingly has nothing to do with the job at hand, such as whether you think that a government-sponsored health plan is feasible for all Americans. Such questions serve several purposes. First, they show just how much you know not only about nursing but about how it relates to health care and other areas. Second, it shows how sure you are of yourself in matters that are important.

Finally, be truthful. No one can be expected to know everything there is to know about nursing or health care, so if you are asked a question and are uncertain of the answer, don't lie. It is much better to tell the truth and admit that you don't know the answer. The interviewer will think all the better of you.

ADVANCEMENT

Okay, you've got the job you wanted. Now, how do you advance? A typical line of advancement in a hospital would be from staff nurse to charge or unit nurse overseeing a unit for a certain shift (nurses ordinarily work three shifts—7:00 A.M. to 3:00 P.M., 3:00 to 11:00 P.M., and 11:00 P.M. to 7:00 A.M.). From there you could move to assistant administrator (there may be several assistant nursing administrators depending on the size of the hospital) or to director of in-service training (to instruct nursing personnel in various new procedures and nursing techniques). And further up the ladder are positions such as director of nursing and assistant administrator for patient services (which might include nursing, inhalation therapy, physical and occupational therapy, dietary or food service, and any other departments having to do with patient service or treatment).

There is also the possibility of going from a position as staff nurse with one hospital to a higher-paying and more responsible position at another facility. It should be noted that for each rung up the ladder of responsibility you might be required to have additional experience and more education. The job may require a master's or Ph.D. degree. You might also advance from staff nurse to one of the advanced practice nurse positions (nurse practitioner, nurse clinician, nurse-midwife, or nurse anesthesiologist), all of which require additional education.

In some cases you might move into the business side of management. Your experience in nursing or as a member of the health care team might qualify you to manage ambulatory care, acute care, home health care, or patient education services. But advancement will depend to a great extent on how nursing develops in the next few years. We will take a look at the future of nursing in Chapter 7.

A LOOK AT THE FUTURE

Trying to predict the future of nursing is like trying to trace your way back home over shifting desert sands. On the one hand, nearly all reliable sources see a glowing future in job opportunities in nursing. The main professional group in nursing, the American Nurses Association, says that hospitals are "having difficulties finding experienced nurses, especially in emergency departments, critical care, labor and delivery, and long-term care." A recent ANA report stated that "reports of emergency department diversions and cancellation of elective surgeries due to short staffing are becoming commonplace."

RECENT CHANGES

However, others are less optimistic about what the future holds for nursing. In his excellent book, *The American Almanac of Jobs and Salaries 1997–1998*, John Wright quotes the ANA to the effect that during the 1980s "salaries for nurses have failed to keep up with inflation in eight of the past seventeen years."

Naturally this had an adverse effect on the profession as a whole, so that by 1980, Wright continues, 25 percent of all nurses had left the field entirely. He quotes *R.N. Magazine* as stating that at the time "only 60 percent of all nurses were working at any given time, creating a vast shortage of nurses from 90,000 to 100,000 nationwide." To ease the situation, some hospitals began to recruit personnel from overseas, especially from the Philippines, Thailand, and other Asian countries that have been the prime source of nursing personnel in recent decades.

Because of this critical shortage of personnel, nurses, like teachers, began to seek work in facilities that paid the most, leaving many economically weaker inner-city hospitals with the biggest shortages. And nurses who only a few years earlier would never have considered unionization began to join unions in record numbers, and at the state level, nurses associations and some nurses employed by public hospitals used the strike— and often the mere threat of a strike—to get higher pay.

With hospitals under governmental and cost-containment pressure to keep the lid on escalating expenses, nursing salaries failed to keep up with those of technical professionals in other fields.

Nurses earned an average of $33,696 in 1991, Wright noted, and it usually took eight to ten years to reach that level. Gradually, however, the larger metropolitan hospitals began to respond to the need for higher salaries, and starting pay for staff registered nurses surpassed $29,000 in five cities— New York, Boston, Los Angeles, Washington, D.C., and Philadelphia. At the same time, salaries for R.N.s in these cities rose to as high as $56,000.

Health care institutions throughout the nation started aggressive recruitment campaigns and wages were increased. The Division of Nursing's national sample survey showed that real average annual salaries of R.N.s working full-time rose from $17,398 in 1980 to $23,166 in 1992, while hospital employment of R.N.s grew steadily by 2 to 3 percent during the 1980s and the early 1990s.

But by the mid-1990s the picture changed as managed care exerted downward pressure on hospital income. In addition, the impact of Medicare prospective payment (payment by category or illness) began to take hold. Providers sought out and put into effect programs to cut costs. As salaries for R.N.s are typically the largest single expenditure for hospitals—averaging about 20 percent of the budget—they were among the first to feel the pinch. Other lower-salaried and lesser-skilled staff were hired as replacements, and R.N. salaries plummeted.

Predictably, hospital employment of R.N.s began to drop, and real wages for hospital R.N.s dropped by roughly a dollar an hour. Jobs for R.N.s working in hospitals dropped, precipitously in areas of the country that were experiencing the most managed-care impact.

Overall, the effect of the changes of the early 1990s was to increase pressure on staff nurses, who now were expected to oversee unlicensed aides while caring for more and sicker patients. Not surprisingly, the changes in the R.N. employment background has resulted in a downturn in the number of R.N.s working in hospitals and increased discontent among those who remain.

THE FUTURE

A recent ANA survey of nurses shows that nearly 55 percent of the nurses surveyed would not recommend nursing as a profession for their children or friends. At the same time, an alarming number of R.N.s are opting out of the field. The 2000 National Sample Survey of Registered Nurses reveals that a record number of nurses (five hundred thousand—more than 18 percent of all nurses employed) who have active licenses are not working in nursing.

According to an ANA survey of nurses across the country, nurses report that they have experienced increased patient loads, increased floating between departments, fewer support services, and increasing demands for compulsory overtime.

Even so, the Bureau of Labor Statistics (BLS), which keeps figures on all categories of employment, says that hospitals, the nation's largest employer of R.N.s, will experience greater demand for R.N.s, but not as much as other sectors of the profession.

While the intensity of nursing care is expected to increase, requiring more nurses per patient, the number of inpatients is not expected to increase very much. Patients are being released earlier, and more and more procedures are being done on an outpatient basis outside of hospitals.

In other areas of employment, the picture is more optimistic. For example, the Bureau of Labor Statistics says that employment in home health care is expected to grow rapidly in response to a rising number of older persons who need health care, but who prefer to receive such care in their own homes.

Likewise, employment of R.N.s in nursing homes is predicted to grow much faster than the average due to the greater number of people in their eighties and nineties, many of whom will require long-term care. Then, too, more and more procedures formerly done only in hospitals are being performed in physicians' offices and clinics, including surgicenters and emergency medical centers.

Since jobs in traditional hospital settings are no longer the only option for R.N.s, they will need to be more flexible. Job opportunities will be good for nurses with advanced education and training, such as nurse practitioners, according to the BLS.

C H A P T E R

8

CONVERSATIONS WITH THOSE IN THE PROFESSION

In this chapter we offer some firsthand conversations that we had recently with people involved in the nursing profession, including students, a director of student support services, a financial aid advisor, and several nurses in various nursing specialties.

Through these conversations we hope that you will gain some additional insights into the nursing profession and that you will be better able to determine your own qualifications for the field.

FOURTH-YEAR STUDENT AT A MIDWESTERN COLLEGE OF NURSING

I am a third-quarter senior student from Doylestown, Pennsylvania. I am completing my studies for a B.S.N. (Bachelor of Science in nursing) here in Illinois and then plan to start in my studies as a family nurse practitioner. I am studying for the D.N. (Doctor of Nursing).

I became interested in nursing because it combines my background in exercise physiology, physical therapy, and cardiac rehabilitation, and it will enable me to help those people in the community with need, as well as to do a little research.

I spent a couple of years working in cardiac rehabilitation and exercise physiology in my hometown. I originally intended to work in an area deprived of health care or in a rehabilitation setting or something combining the two.

I am twenty-six, single, and because I like rock climbing and skiing, I visited Colorado and really enjoyed the area. I would like to settle there for another reason, too. The role of advanced practice nurses is more autonomous in Colorado than in most states, so I feel that once I get my degree, I'd really be able to put it to good use there.

It's my understanding that if you open a clinic in Colorado, a physician will come once a month to review your records and make sure you're making proper documentation. So for all intents and purposes, I'd be practicing pretty much on my own. I'd be able to prescribe medications, see patients, and take patient histories. I would not be able to do surgery or admit patients to hospitals. I could become certified as an acute-care nurse practitioner and my role would be in the emergency room and in surgery assisting, but I would not be able to admit or do surgery.

After I get my degree as a nurse practitioner, I'd have to be certified. I believe that Colorado and Illinois have reciprocal agreements, but even so I'd probably try for certification in Colorado. I could take my licensing exam in Illinois and still practice in Colorado and be licensed to practice in that state. You're not limited to just one state in which you can practice.

My studies have been what I expected, and I am learning a great deal about pathophysiology and pharmacology. I'm also learning about the community, which I did not anticipate. This school is more sociology-based—more than it's medically or disease-based. And I am learning how various things affect the family and the community—the area of public health nursing.

I don't find the curriculum difficult, but it is time-consuming. On a typical Monday through Wednesday, I am in class from 8:00 A.M. to 4:00 P.M. and I have two clinical days from 7:00 A.M. to 3:30 P.M. on Thursday and Friday at the hospital, with a medical-surgical class called "Health Care of the Individual." We learn about diseases. If it's a cancerous disease, we try to find out what caused it, what interventions can be made, and what nursing care is expected.

Education is particularly sticky. Even though you may do well in your studies, how to educate the family about illness is more problematic. In pharmacology, nurses are seen as the last preventive barrier for the patient. In other words, they are the last to see the medication and what it is intended to do for the patient. We try to make sure that the patient does not have any adverse effects.

This quarter we'll spend ten weeks in the surgical area, including the medical-surgical floor, the operating room, outpatient surgery, and others. Next quarter we go to obstetrics-gynecology, and we'll be there for ten weeks. I will have to do a psychological test first—that's an elective. Ordinarily, we do not get any exposure in this area.

In the medical-surgical area, you are not in the intensive care unit, but the patients come right to ICU and that's where they go. From the medical-surgical floor in my first quarter, I went to an AIDS floor. The patients there are critically ill. They don't need constant monitoring like the patients in the ICU, but if something life-threatening were to happen, they would go right back to the ICU.

I would prefer to work in a community clinic. Personally I do not want to work in a hospital. I like the autonomy of being out in the community—not that you don't have interaction with your patients in the hospital, but in the clinic you can develop a better relationship on a long-term basis. As a nurse practitioner, I would see my own patients, year in and year out, whereas hospital work is more short-term and intensive, and there's more management instead of direct patient care. You do care for patients, but you are managing the care for others, for example, if the patient has to go to physical therapy or the lab.

I'll need two to three more years after I get my bachelor's degree to practice as a nurse practitioner, depending on if I can do this full-time or part-time, and if clinical rotations open up. There are only so many clinical centers that you can go to.

Right now I'm working for the Chicago Center doing clinical research on drug studies. I work weekends at the center, and then on Monday and Tuesday I'll usually work till about 5:30 P.M., about twenty hours total, and then I'll go home and study. I usually study until about 10:30 P.M. and then go to sleep. I work to get nursing experience and earn some money.

Nursing is an expensive program. My loan for a year's study at this school is $25,000, which includes tuition, room, and board. But what the school determines is adequate for rent really is not. That's why I work. I do, however, manage to have some social life on Saturday evenings.

There are thirty-two students in my class and six of them are men. This is something I just don't think about. You simply go through your day and that's it. I have friends, both male and female. In school I really enjoy the learning, especially the science classes—medical pharmacology and patho-physiology. I also value the friendships I have formed here at school. We've spent a lot of time together.

I am looking forward to practicing as a family nurse practitioner. I already have a Bachelor of Science degree and am going back for another bachelor's degree. I did four years of work at Pennsylvania State University before coming here. You were once able to enroll as a graduate student and go right into the nurse practitioner program here, but they did away with that. Now it's a separate program.

To be accepted at this school, you must have completed two years of undergraduate work and then you have to enroll here and finish up a B.S.N. degree. Most of the people here have a four-year degree, have been work-ing for a while, and have decided they want to go into nursing. They came here because there is a summer start program, where you can finish up in a year and four months even though technically it's a two-year program. I had many chemical biology courses as an undergraduate, as well as anatomy, physiology, psychology, sociology, and behavioral science. You also need human development from birth to death. This is required in many schools. Sociology and psychology are also good since the trend in nursing seems to be going to community-based practices.

You have to be caring to succeed in nursing. You really have to want to help your patients and feel comfortable with them, so you need to be able to communicate openly. If you really want to use nursing to its fullest, you need a good science background in high school and college. There are so many routes you can take in nursing school. If you have a strong desire to learn, you will succeed.

I believe one of the principal reasons I came here is that having a nurs-ing degree is going to open up a lot of avenues—research, cardiac rehabil-itation, community nursing, hospital, advanced practice. There is almost no limit to what you can do.

FOURTH-YEAR STUDENT IN BACHELOR OF NURSING PROGRAM

I am from Elmhurst, a Chicago suburb; twenty-five years old; and a senior in the bachelor of nursing program. Originally I did my undergraduate work at a state university and had no idea of what I wanted to do. I thought I was interested in nutrition, so I got my degree in that field at Colorado State University. Then I decided that it was not what I really wanted to do. I had taken gross anatomy, diet, and disease and wanted to do more with the patient than merely nutrition—this seemed too isolated for me. I wanted to be more involved in something concerning the human body and all of its systems, so I started volunteering at a small community hospital in Fort Collins, Colorado. I worked in the emergency room and loved the fast pace of the place. That was when I decided to go into nursing. That was two years ago.

What's interesting about this school is that it offers a bachelor's degree, but you come in as a junior. You must complete two years of college and certain prerequisites before you are accepted, but there is no associate nursing program. In high school you need many chemistry, biology, and math courses—there's a lot of math in nursing. You also should be exposed to patients by volunteering in a hospital, a community center, or a nursing home.

Since I had already received my bachelor's degree, I didn't want to have to go through another four years of school to get my nursing degree. I chose Rush because it has a wonderful reputation and I was able to apply the courses that I had taken at Colorado State University.

I find this school a lot harder than I thought it would be. Usually at the beginning of the week we start at 8:00 A.M. with lecture sessions followed by some group discussion. We have a facilitator to guide us in the discussion. If the discussion is on critical thinking, we go through all the points of a case study and do research on issues that we don't have answers for. This helps us in working with patients because you have to know where to get help if you are uncertain of what to do. So we do a lot of problem-solving in these discussions, and in our classes we learn the basic concepts and theories of nursing. We have clinical work with patients in the hospital two days a week both here at Rush and at Rush–North Shore in Skokie, Illinois. We also work in clinics for our home health nursing and community nursing courses at a shelter for homeless people who are too sick to go out, but not sick enough to be in a hospital. And we visit psychiatric patients' homes and learn how to communicate with them. We have learned not only the basics of nursing, but also how to assess vital signs and how to assess the patients' impact on their families and the environment in which they live.

Right now, in addition to my schooling, I have a part-time job working at Elmhurst Hospital on the cardiac floor. It's a cardiac step-down unit. I like it because I can utilize my knowledge of nutrition. This is a unit where we get patients in postoperative open-heart surgery who have just come out of the ICU. When we get them they are still very sick, but not sick enough to be in a critical care unit. Others have had angioplasties or cardiac catheterization; some have irregular heartbeat or arrhythmia. I do this in my free time on Fridays and Saturdays.

I am in school Monday through Thursday. Monday and Tuesday I have my lectures, and Wednesday and Thursday I have clinicals, where I work with patients. Friday and Saturday I work my part-time job. Working even part-time is frowned upon here, especially during our first year, when we get all the theories and knowledge, and during our last year, when we build on these basic concepts. So it's tough and you don't have much of a life of your own.

At Rush, since we have already taken our basic sciences—anatomy, chemistry, and biology—we can concentrate on pharmacology and pathophysiology, which are more practical science courses, and on our assessment course, where we learn how to assess the health of our patients. This includes how to give shots, how to insert a catheter, and how to start an IV. In the second year, we take the skills that we have learned and apply them in patient care settings.

I have just started my labor and delivery rotation. I didn't think that I was going to like it. I haven't been around children that much, but I have fallen in love with this area, so I am not so certain that I will still go into cardiac care as I had originally planned. Right now I am in the middle of my pediatric care, neonatal care, and labor and delivery rotations.

In our first year, we were in class every day from 8:00 A.M. to 5:00 P.M. This does not include studying, just classes and discussion. I would then go home and would study another four or five hours daily and most of the weekend.

My nursing class is my family. I see my classmates more than I do my family! And, for the most part, I have been with the same classmates throughout my studies here. Now in our senior year, we are able to add some electives, so I chose a critical care class. I love this class.

At this stage, I know that I like the fast pace and turnover of medical intensive care—cardiac, critical care, and ICU. Patients move in and out in a matter of a day or two, whereas some of the other areas are slower and not as challenging. When you are in an intensive care or a labor and delivery unit, you are dealing with one type of care, whereas on some of the other floors, you are involved with several kinds of patients—all with different problems—at one time. Personally, I like to get to know my patients better and to know their good days and their bad days. Also, I like to get to know their families. In critical care you are responsible for about three patients, whereas on a general floor you could be involved with eight to ten patients. I would rather be able to concentrate more on a few patients and be able to give them all of my attention.

The next step is to graduate and to get my bachelor's degree in nursing, then get certified and take my state boards (a computer-generated test). You get the results in two to three weeks. If you pass you get your R.N. designation. If you specialize, you need to go back to school. So if I want to go into intensive care, I could go directly into it with my bachelor's degree as an R.N. But I do plan to go back to school to get my master's. I don't know exactly which way I will go because I am still not sure of what area of nursing is my forte. But once I have established myself on a unit and know that that's what I really want to do, then I'll go for my master's.

I think that my future is being laid out right now in the form of the laws that are being enacted. And I know that there are a lot of issues in nursing right now that will affect me, such as cutting back of licensed personnel and giving more nursing duties to unlicensed personnel. Nurses are doing more of the management of the unlicensed personnel. I thought I would be much more involved in direct patient care, not supervising the work of other personnel. The thought of having someone else work under my license makes me uneasy, and it is something I was not aware of before, when I first came into nursing. I would like to see nursing go back to where it used to be, that is, being more compassionate and caring.

I had thought of going into advanced practice nursing, but I am not sure which areas of APN I want to go into. Someone coming into nursing really needs to determine what he or she wants out of nursing. If you want to go beyond being an R.N. or staff nurse, you need to have your bachelor's degree, and then you need to look at what your long-term goals are before choosing a program.

Working part-time has helped me a great deal. It's given me the confidence I need in dealing with my patients. I am applying the skills I have acquired at school to the patients I work with.

ASSISTANT DEAN FOR STUDENT SERVICES

Our school is an upper-division college. Our students do their first two years at any university or college. There are certain prerequisites that they must have prior to their coming here. They could have an associate's (two-year) degree or they could come directly from a university after two years of study.

There are several two-year nursing programs where students finish with their associate's degree and then can be certified as an R.N.

In our admissions requirements, we are looking for a grade point average above a 2.75 on a 4.0 scale. In addition, students need to have certain prerequisites: organic chemistry and microbiology. There are two other four-year bachelor's programs in the area; they are attached to full-service universities. Students can get their prerequisites there and go on for their bachelor's degree, or they can come here for the nursing courses they will need to get their bachelor's degree. They can take the humanities, the biological sciences, and the behavioral science courses at the university where they are studying. Or they may be going to a liberal arts college with no nursing program and after a couple of years of study decide that they want to go into nursing. Also, they may go to a community college in the area and then come here for their final two years and still obtain their bachelor's degree in nursing.

We get many students who have been working in other careers and then changed their minds and decided that they wanted to go into nursing. This has been the trend for the past ten years or so. We are getting more and more second-career people. Half of our starting class this year came from other fields. The students we now get are different from those who were going to nursing school twenty years ago. They are older, second-career people, many with children and many single parents. More than half have bachelor's degrees, and others have master's degrees. In many cases they were not fulfilled in their careers and were frustrated.

Recently *Time* magazine said that nursing was listed as one of the ten top growth professions. Nursing was number two, so many second-career students tell themselves that this looks like a pretty good field in a society where many are getting used to having six, seven, or eight jobs in a lifetime. It's not like it used to be when people worked in the same place for thirty or thirty-five years. People are looking for security in a profession, and they think that nursing offers that to them. Then there are the opportunities offered in advanced practice nursing, where they say that nursing is not just confined to the bedside anymore. Now they can be independent nurse practitioners. In most cases APNs work collaboratively with someone, but they don't have to.

There are approximately two hundred students in the undergraduate program, and we also offer a master's degree program, a D.N. (Doctor of Nursing) program, and a D.N.Sc. (Doctor of Nursing Science) program. In these programs students do original research—they are primarily for anyone who wants to work in academia or in basic research.

Other admissions requirements are for students to write a few short paragraphs on their career goals and what they have done in health care. This gives us a good idea of how serious or motivated the student is. We also require recommendations from their teachers. We get many applications for each available spot. We look at applicants' portfolios and decide if they will be accepted or not.

Once they are accepted, their chances of completing the program are excellent. We have had less than 5 percent attrition in the last two years. The students work in basic sciences, chemistry, microbiology, anatomy, and physiology.

When they come here they are doing pathophysiology and pharmacology, which are applied sciences. Then they do everything that is connected with their clinical work, such as health assessments. They also are getting concept courses in nursing such as communications and ethics. Then they get skill labs in connection with their clinical work. They are exposed to the clinical areas to see patients almost from the very start in their first quarter. It is much less than what they will get later, but it's a start. In their first quarter they are in a clinical setting for a few hours. Training is not just hospital-based anymore. They're out in the community at various clinics because that's where the jobs are going to be. This is hard for students to grasp because they are indoctrinated to the likes of "ER" and "Presidio Med" on television.

Now things are moving toward outpatient care. When a patient comes in for minor surgery, that patient is in and out of the hospital within twenty-three hours. This used to be more than a thousand-bed hospital. We now fill about 550 beds. Every other hospital is the same.

Initially, in the first quarter, there are probably twenty-four to twenty-eight hours of class and lab time. The next quarter it drops a little, so that students are not yet being fully exposed to the clinical specialties. But by the third quarter, they are in clinics about fifteen hours a week, two days a week, either in the hospital or away. Class time is now cut down a lot, because students are spending their time primarily in clinical practice. But it's still a lot of hours per week that they are spending on any given activity.

Many students do work part-time and are married. A few have tried going to school and working full-time, but they finished miserably.

It is not easy to measure an applicant's motivation or affinity for work. You don't always know what you're getting, although the schools they come from can often be an indication. Logically, if one student comes from a large university and another from a local college, and they both have the same grade point average, you pick the one from the school that has a higher standing.

We have an admissions committee that selects the students. Most of the students stay on in nursing. Some nurses go into an M.B.A. program because they wish to combine nursing with business management. This is the most popular choice outside of nursing.

There are about forty-three thousand R.N.s at all levels in Illinois, and less than 1 percent of those have their doctorate. We require two years of college, but others may have lower requirements. A master's will soon become a requirement to get credentials as an advanced practice nurse.

Students should know about the changes in the profession as the result of health care trends. There has been tremendous pressure for the last few years, particularly by managed care, for the profession to change in an effort to deliver more cost-effective care. Nursing is in a good position to do this in that we have always been cost-effective health care deliverers. Opportunities legitimately given by law will expand the number of opportunities in different settings. It's not just a choice between "Presidio Med" or "ER." People who want to work will find that patients are much more acutely ill. They are sicker. These are the ones that are being hospitalized today. No longer can you say "I don't feel well" and have your doctor put you in the hospital for a couple of weeks.

With a bachelor's degree, there are more outpatient opportunities—working for clinics, at community centers, and as case managers in managed health care. All of these outpatient settings used in the old days are changing. New nurses go there now to get their year of experience, and only then are they ready to go into the outpatient center. They never had to train anybody. And this is not just going to happen because there are not the jobs in inpatient nursing that can train nurses. Outpatient settings will be responsible for training nurses. Nursing schools are responding to health care trends and are working with outpatient clinics to help them to be ready for training.

For example, one of the things that we've accounted for is in the area of psychiatry—the number of psychiatry inpatients is shrinking, as is just about every other segment of hospital nursing. A lot of our experiences are now for undergraduate outpatient exposure—working at the state hospital, or as a threshold for a community psychiatric organization, for example, the Council for Jewish Elderly. They have an Alzheimer's day care program and it involves home visits.

Everything is in flux—where students train, how they are employed, and so forth. It's hard to know which direction to go in; so many students change direction once they get out of school. They find that some particular branch of nursing might not be quite what they anticipated. They might start out in pediatrics, working with small children, and end up in psychiatry.

Tuition varies from school to school. We are a private institution and below the midpoint in tuition for a private school. Many private colleges are more expensive. We can't compete with public nursing schools, but you have to be a resident of the state in which the school is located. And even at a state public school, the tuition can be close to $15,000 a year for out-of-state residents. We've tried to hold our tuition as low as we can, at about $10,000 a year. Even so, most of our graduate students are part-time because they are all working. Many hospitals offer tuition reimbursement. That is something all students should look into when they finish nursing school.

ASSISTANT DIRECTOR OF STUDENT FINANCIAL AID

Technically we are a four-year school simply because we do award a bachelor's degree, but students must do their first two years at another college. This is an unusual setup because normally the community colleges or universities offer the first two years. Students take their social science, humanities, and science electives at the other school before they transfer here.

Right now our tuition is $3,418 per quarter, or $10,254 a year, and we have two hundred students. About 85 percent of them receive some kind of financial aid.

The process involves "reapplication" for federal funding. Although it's a federal application, it is used to determine the amount of state and institutional aid a student will get. The application goes to a federal processor. We get the results in about four to six weeks and based on the results of that application, we can determine how much federal, state, and institutional aid a student can receive.

If the student wants to receive institutional aid from Rush, they must fill out another application and provide parental information, even if they are living independently of such income. This aid consists of scholarships and loans that do not accrue interest until after the student graduates.

We do offer a work-study program that is another form of financial aid. We get the results and we put together a financial package that tells the students what type and/or amount of aid they will receive. If the students find that it's not enough, they can contact us and we will review their files to see if there's anything else we can give them. Usually, it will be in the form of additional loans. We try to give the students the best aid—scholarships and loans that do not accrue interest right away.

Generally, we award a minimum of $5,500 in a Stafford federal loan to nursing students and $8,500 to graduate nursing students per year. You can assume that all undergraduates will receive $5,500 in Stafford loans. Some students might need additional loans—federal loans that don't accrue interest or institutional loans that do not accrue interest right away. After this, they could receive a federal unsubsidized loan that would accrue interest while they are in school.

Generally, we award students a combination of loans and scholarships. Nonetheless, most students carry a debt of at least $11,000 when they finish here, but this does not accrue interest until they get their bachelor's degree.

How much the student receives depends upon tuition and a living allowance. If the student lives at home, that would be a lesser amount ($535 a month). For students living on campus or who have their own apartment, it would be anywhere from $675 to $1,035 a month. Out of this, they would have to pay transportation, rent, utilities—any living expenses that they might have. If a student has a crisis that results in expenses he or she has not budgeted for, that student can appeal and receive additional aid, but most often this consists of loans. All students receive a living allowance.

Students submit applications to the federal processor. They may or may not be eligible for scholarships and loans. But we determine their eligibility based on the same standards for all students. A student may not have had very much income from the previous year, and this is what we look at. And another student might have had a lot of income and they might have a lot of assets. Whatever their assets or financial picture, that is what determines how much they get. Some students are eligible for state scholarships this year, which is $4,000 from the state per year. So they can receive federal scholarships and loans, state scholarships, and institutional scholarships. Our statements in the financial aid handbook apply to other private institutions, except for the private institutional scholarships, which vary from school to school.

It is very important that students apply for aid as soon as possible. The application will ask for the previous year's income, so if they filed a return, they can go ahead and apply. If they have not or will not file by April 15, and if their parents have not filed, I would suggest that the student estimate what he or she made in the previous year. The federal processor will ask us to go back later and get those tax forms and verify the amounts. I ask them to estimate, because if they are eligible for the Illinois State Scholarship, the application must be in by June 1.

They should get those forms filled out and get documents with instructions on how to proceed; sometimes they will have to provide us with income tax returns, proof of Social Security earnings, and so forth. They'll get mail from the federal processor and from us. Once we see the results, we know what other documents they have to submit. It's important that they answer all mail because a lot of times we cannot award aid of any kind unless our files are complete. And if this information is received too late, students may miss out on scholarship aid for that year.

If students have no means of meeting the tuition and living expenses, we can help them if they have applied for financial aid and have given us all the documents that we need. The worst-case scenario is that they might get all loans instead of scholarships and loans.

It is also important to have a good credit record. The bank might turn down students who are otherwise eligible for aid if they have a bad credit record. That's not something we can control.

Students should also realize that they don't have to wait to be accepted before applying for financial aid. They can fill out all the required forms before they are accepted. The application will ask what schools they have applied to. Students can ask that the results go to six different schools, so that even if they have not yet made up their minds, we can still make an award for them; they don't have to wait six to eight weeks before applying. If a student decides not to come here, we just ignore the results.

Probably 80 to 85 percent of our students are from the Chicago area. Tuition is the same for all students.

GERONTOLOGICAL NURSE PRACTITIONER

I started working at Rush after I received my bachelor's degree in nursing. My first job was on a surgical step-down floor, where patients are sicker than they are on an average floor. Many had been in surgical intensive care. From there I went to home care, which is what I was doing when I finished my master's degree in gerontological nursing. That qualified me to take the certifying exam for nurse practitioner. Ever since starting in nursing, I had wanted to be an NP because I knew they practiced a little more independently than general nurses. I've been in my current position here at the Center for the Elderly for two years.

Whether or not you work with a doctor depends on the state. In Illinois, unfortunately, the nurse practitioner (NP) is not recognized separately from other nursing roles. So in Illinois we do not have special licensure privileges as a nurse practitioner. In other states you practice within the scope of the nurse practice act, and usually this entails working in collaboration with a physician. I will probably stay on here, though. My husband is self-employed and I am happy with my work situation. Hopefully, this will continue. Also, there are good opportunities for advanced practice nurses in Illinois.

Although my responsibilities are circumscribed by law, I do have more responsibility according to my employers. Since the nurse practitioner is not recognized separately, I function under an arrangement I work out with the physician. For the most part, I have been happy with this, but it can be frustrating at times.

Among the things I do are take complete histories, give physicals, do patient education, and manage many patients in health and wellness, chronic disease management, and home visits.

I also supervise a group of lay community health workers, who have been trained by the physician I work with and by the NP who had the job before me. They function as educated neighbors to isolated elderly in the

Mexican enclave in which I work. Most of my patients are Latino, and there is a much higher incidence of diabetes among Hispanic elderly than in the general population. But other than that, the health problems we see are pretty typical of all people. We get many patients with heart problems, high cholesterol, arthritis, and so forth.

My specialty is the care of older people. In the office, however, I work with various age groups, including teenagers who are not working. My patients are primarily women. Generally, women take better care of themselves. This is true of older patients as well. I work in this clinic, which is affiliated with Rush, to meet the specific needs of people in this community.

I grew up in South America. I was born in Colombia, raised in Ecuador, and then spent a year in Honduras. My parents were missionaries. We did have access to physicians, but the people I was most familiar with since I was a little girl were nurses. As a high school senior and at the start of college, I considered medicine briefly, but for several reasons I did not pursue this. It takes years to complete, and I didn't have the self-confidence or the exposure in knowing people who were doctors, so it was kind of a foreign area for me. Nursing was something I was more comfortable with.

In a health professions seminar—a pre-nursing course—that I took in my second year at Wheaton College, they made sure that you had some exposure to nursing. The course was designed to discuss health care issues, and during spring break we went out and observed what went on in our field of practice. There were people taking the course who planned to go into medicine, physical therapy, and occupational therapy.

Going through nursing school, my most positive experiences were with older patients—my first clinical exposure was a very nice home on the North Side, where I did not have a positive experience with younger patients. This has been a constant in my nursing experience. So when I applied for a job, I identified the place best known for the nursing care and education of older people, which was here at the Center for the Jewish Elderly. This was my first position. Rush is the one and only hospital I've worked for, and it has traditionally been very supportive of nursing education, including advanced practice. So as long as I was working full-time, it would pay my tuition for up to six hours, or two courses. That was a good way for me to get my education.

I figured out that it cost between $16,000 and $18,000 to get my master's degree, and I didn't have to pay for any of it. That was great.

For the near future, I would very much like to continue as a geronto-logical NP. I like the patient population. I enjoy using my Spanish.

In nursing you must enjoy doing what you do. Nursing is changing with medicine. Fewer patients are entering the hospital, and those who do are staying for shorter periods. Those patients that we do see in hospitals tend to be very ill, and more of the care given in the hospital will be at the intensive care level. Beyond that, care will be given at home.

You must be able to relate to many different people at various educational levels. You will care for people with advanced degrees and others who are very bright but never had a chance to study. As to working with patients, you never know how they're going to react. It depends upon what situations they find themselves in. For example, a patient with a basic health problem might be more upset than one having a life-and-death problem. You can't assume much when you are dealing with people—you must figure them out individually.

As to the academic requirements of nursing school, it helps to be good in math and science. You have to take biology and chemistry. The math comes in handy in making your basic calculations—in figuring medications and IVs. I find nurses to be notoriously poor in math and usually decent in science, but it helps to be good in both. Social science is needed because it takes a lot of psychology and people skills to succeed in nursing. It also helps if you are in a liberal arts program. So nursing is an art and a science.

There are three ways to qualify for the R.N. licensure exam. The first is to go to an accredited hospital school of nursing that is not college-based—a three-year diploma program. Probably the most well-known program in this area is St. Francis Hospital in Evanston, but these programs are really fading from the scene.

The second way is the associate's degree, which is a two-year program, college-based, usually with a community college. Finally, there is the bachelor of science degree in nursing, which is a typical four-year college degree. Nursing has debated ad nauseam what the entry level of nursing should be without reaching a decision. So here at Rush we hire people with all three kinds of educational backgrounds. It depends a great deal on the nursing supply.

There is more agreement on educational requirements for advanced practice nursing. In the past you could be an APN without getting a master's degree, but this is no longer true. People without the master's degree are being grandfathered in, but now a master's degree is required.

Traditionally, NPs have been trained in health, wellness, and long-term health care, and they have tended to work in the community. Clinical nurse specialists are trained more for in-hospital management of patients, specializing in pulmonary or cardiology patients, for instance. But that's changing because of the new emphasis on primary care. Many hospitals today want NPs and not just clinical nurse specialists. So many of the nurses today are taking classes to qualify to take the NP exam. You will find NPs working wherever—from community centers to emergency rooms to ICUs—there are those with the title of clinical nurse specialist who do not have advanced training. It can be an adopted title, but that does not necessarily indicate the level of competence. The NP has several options—gerontology, pediatrics, family and community care.

To decide what area of nursing is for you, get some exposure to various nursing specialties throughout your basic training. You might have some idea of what way you want to go beforehand, or you may not have a clue. If you don't know which way you want to go, you should be open to all avenues of nursing. If you do know, you should try to get more exposure in those areas of greatest interest to you and let your instructors know of your desire to have more exposure in a given area of nursing. If, for instance, you know that you would like to work with children and you are doing your various rotations, you might want to concentrate more in the area of pediatric psychiatric nursing. If you're doing a community health rotation, you might want to work in a place that deals with children. And if you are doing general nursing, you might want to have more exposure to areas where there are children.

If you are thinking about going into nursing and are entering college, you should be open to various areas of nursing specialization. You don't know enough about the various options open to you and you don't know yourself well enough to know which way to go.

You might wind up in an area that you don't like as much as you thought you would. If, for instance, you are a very hands-on, skills-oriented person, you might want to go into surgical nursing at the operating-room level and not just take care of patients before or after surgery. If you like more dialogue and ongoing relationships with patients, you might consider psychiatric nursing or home care.

The way nursing education is today, I think it's still important to put in a few years in hospitals no matter what your goal. In the hospital, you are working with other nurses from whom you can learn and receive support. And when you come out of school, no matter how good your program, you will have had only so much exposure to the various areas of nursing and still have a lot to learn. So working in a hospital with other nurses is the quickest way to learn various nursing skills—those hands-on skills and patient assessment skills that you might not have gotten in school. It's difficult to go directly from school to home care, where you are expected to function much more independently, and it's important to get a certain amount of experience before you go on in your education. And there are schools that urge you to get more and more education and not worry about experience. I don't really agree with this. To get the most out of your advanced nursing training, you need a certain level of experience.

It also depends on your age. Many people going into nursing today are older and coming into nursing as a second career. They've already been professionals in other careers, so entering nursing, they are already professionals to a certain degree, but they need specific nursing skills. However, if you are entering nursing right from high school, you have to go to college and then graduate. You are learning to be a professional while you attend nursing school.

Finally, you should be aware of some of the problems that nurses must face. There is some confusion as to precisely what nursing is. For example, there's confusion as to how dependent nurses should be on physicians. And there is also the notion that we are not professional ourselves, but function under the guidance of a physician. This is a subject of some disagreement. When you analyze the meaning of professional, nursing does have some problems. This starts with agreement as to what nursing education should entail. We have come a long way, but we have a lot of work to do. We also have trouble in being directly reimbursed for services. At present, we are not directly reimbursed either as staff nurses or as advanced practice nurses, and our services are billed as part of the physician's services.

When a patient gets a bill from the hospital and sees that a room costs $750 a day, that patient is not paying just for the room but for nursing services received. If nursing services are not recognized by insurance companies or by the government through Medicare, that limits what we can do. The states where NPs function most independently are those where NPs are needed the most for patient care and where managed care has been more aggressive—such as California, Oregon, and Washington. There they recognized early on the economies in health care that could be realized through the use of NPs—that health care services could be provided for more people at lower costs.

NPs traditionally have been employed in medically underserved areas, and the Veterans Administration has always been a good employer for NPs. Nurse practitioners are just beginning to make inroads into areas where patients have good insurance.

SUPERVISOR OF OPERATING ROOM NURSES IN A MIDSIZED HOSPITAL

I am a graduate of Concordia Nursing School in Manila in the Philippines. I finished my schooling in 1969 and came to Norwegian American Hospital as a graduate nurse. I took my state boards in the United States in 1971.

I started my nursing career in the United States at St. Anne's Hospital on the west side of Chicago in an exchange program, came to Norwegian in 1974, and have been here ever since. I started as a nurse in surgery. We have five operating rooms including cystoscopy. We average fifteen to twenty-five patients a day.

We built a whole new operating room area on the west side of the hospital, which was finished several years ago. When I started, we worked out of the old operating room suite, which was located in approximately the same area as the new one and which now serves as our offices and a ten-bed recovery room.

To work in the operating room you must be an R.N. and preferably certified as a certified operating room nurse (CNOR), but not all of our OR nurses are certified. This does not mean that they are not qualified. It's more like a status symbol, but you still have to be certified in OR and must take a certification exam and be a member of the American Operating Room Nurses' Association. We have six R.N.s and five certified surgical technologists (CSTs), who are not nurses.

It takes at least two to three years to become a good operating room nurse. When we hire someone for the operating room, we want someone with at least three to four years of experience. We don't want to hire people with no experience since we don't have the staff to train them. We also look for someone who can take the pressure of working in surgery, someone who is calm and doesn't easily panic. Some nurses just can't stand the sight of blood or viewing the patient's organs, and that's not the kind of thing that you will ordinarily face on the nursing floor. You also need special skills to be an intensive care nurse. You have to be well versed in reading EKGs and you need trauma experience.

This is a high-tension department. In a complicated operation you have to make some split-second decisions—and there is a need to adapt to the surgeon's personality. Some surgeons will holler and scream over simple things. Others are very nice and relaxed under stress or when there are complications. And some surgeons are very temperamental, and when they face tense situations they get upset and start throwing things and screaming. You have to deal with these personalities.

Our hospital is a small community hospital, but we handle a lot of cases that are comparable to those handled in a large university hospital. True, we don't do open-heart surgery or anything like that, but we do the simpler cardiovascular cases, such as a femoral bypass. Compared to other hospitals in the area, we do a lot of cases, primarily obstetrics and gynecology, but we are also doing a lot of laparoscopic work and cholecystectomies. Previously, to remove, say, a gallbladder or an appendix, you would have to open up the patient. Now all the manipulations are done through a scope. You remove the gallbladder or appendix through an incision of roughly an inch. Last year we removed about forty-five gallbladders.

And when we did a gallbladder removal in the past, it would take a patient maybe a week to recover. Today the patient goes home the following day and can go back to work in less than a week. There is less pain, less trauma to the patient, and less expense.

In 1991 I was promoted to Assistant Nursing Clinical Coordinator in the OR and became Director of OR Nursing in 1994 when the position opened up.

I still work on some cases, but I do it for my own benefit. I don't want to forget my knowledge or OR nursing skills. If you don't practice these skills in the OR you tend to forget them. So about half of my time is spent in surgery and the balance in administration—scheduling the nurses, running meetings, and so forth. Many hospitals have a director of OR who is strictly administrative and concerned primarily with budgets, scheduling, training, and so forth. In the smaller hospital, we don't have the manpower to do administration only.

I love OR work. I like to scrub and I still want to see cases. Every day is a new learning experience, and there is new technology that you must understand. Like I said before, we do an awful lot by laparoscopy these days. We also do ovarian cystectomies. Before, if there was a tumor in the ovaries, you had to open everything, but now this can be done through laparoscopy. Today we also don't do as much suturing of openings. For example, to close a bowel, it used to take ten to fifteen minutes to do all the suturing. Now we can do this in less than two minutes with a new kind of staple. It's easier on the patient, too, and there is less chance for infection. It's certainly a lot different from when I started in 1974. Surgery is a good field for a person with the right experience and the right personality.

If you are an OR nurse, you will never have a problem finding work because OR nurses are in great demand. You can find work in surgicenters, where they do nothing but surgery, as well as in hospitals. An OR nurse with hospital experience has excellent qualifications for the surgicenters.

OR nurses make more than regular nurses do. Our nurses have on-call privileges. They work five days a week, but once or twice a week they take call—either at home or at the hospital—and they may have to come in for certain cases.

Average wages for OR nurses in this area are between $40,000 and $45,000 a year. A beginner will average $35,000 to $40,000 a year, and it goes up from there. There are some nurses here who make more than $80,000 a year.

You see a variety of cases, each requiring special skills. It's a very challenging job.

PRE- AND POSTOPERATIVE PATIENT NURSE AT A LARGE MEDICAL CENTER

I work with pre- and postoperative patients at a large medical center in Chicago. I was there full-time for nineteen years and am still working there part-time in the surgical area. To do this type of nursing, you have to be an R.N. licensed in Illinois. To get started, for several months I worked a preceptorship under the review of a supervisor who was helping me.

I have an associate's degree in nursing from a community college—a two-year program—and started working immediately after that in 1978.

Before that I had always wanted to get into nursing but I was discouraged. So instead I worked for about ten years first as a secretary, then dispatcher, for a large motor coach company that transported handicapped children. I decided to go back to school to become a nurse because of my oldest daughter's cardiac problems.

When I started in night school in 1971, I wanted to go into surgical nursing, because people come in for surgery and usually go home in short order. This is as opposed to general nursing, where you are dealing with patients who may have chronic or long-term conditions such as arthritis, heart problems, or diabetes.

Because I work in a large teaching hospital we have some very interesting cases, and it is an ongoing education for me. There are hospitals much closer to where I live, but these are community hospitals that do not have the diversity of patients that you see here. It is a challenge working not only with different people and with a wide variety of cases, but with many different doctors, too. It's a good exchange that keeps me on my toes.

But nursing is changing a lot; an associate's degree is no longer sufficient. You need at least a bachelor's degree . . . possibly even additional education. I continued to take nursing courses even after I got my associate's degree. And I probably will go back to school now because the nurse's role is changing. Now the nurse is responsible for managing the patient, and you have more of an administrative role instead of a role in patient care. You are more of a coordinator of health care and an advocate for the patient. Aides and assistants are doing more of the things that the nurse used to do, such as bathing patients. In some ways this helps the nurse, but in others it gives him or her more to do. You are responsible for patient care, and if an aide or assistant makes a mistake, it's your fault.

So you realize that you will be working more in an administrative capacity. You will be the patient's advocate, the one who intercedes for the patient to make sure that the care is correct, that doctor's orders are being followed, and that the follow-through is appropriate. Similarly in home care, there is a need for a well-rounded nurse to take care of the patient at home and to follow through on his or her needs. Either way you have to be able to assess the patient.

If I had it to do over again, I'd do it exactly the same. Possibly, if I had begun at a younger age, I'd have become a physician, but this was a difficult thing to do when I was young, and I was not encouraged to go this route.

To succeed in nursing you need a B.S. degree. And it helps if you have a lot of compassion for your fellow man and are willing to work long hours. You may have to work more than five days a week or you may have to work Saturday and Sunday. You may also be scheduled to work holidays.

Often, if you are a graduate of a teaching hospital, you may be able to get started in a teaching hospital. There are many opportunities, despite all the downsizing you hear about. Managed care seems to be coming up strong as a source of jobs.

To find out if you will like nursing, I advise any student to work as a candy striper or volunteer. Sometimes when you actually see what has to be done, you might not want to do it, and vice versa. Nursing can be very satisfying, and it's good to see young people doing volunteer work and to see them come along. This is good experience. And in the hospital, people are not the cheerful, happy beings that they might normally be. People who are sick can be disagreeable, and you might not be able to deal with that. And when you are a patient in a hospital, you are no longer in control. You are subject to the conditions of the hospital and you can become grumpy and hard to deal with, so you take it out on your nurse. But when the patients start to recover, they go through many changes and usually are easier to deal with.

There are so many aspects of nursing that you can go into—teaching, research, office jobs, and all of the other hospital specialties. If you do go into nursing and find yourself in something that is not what you thought it would be, you can always change to some other field of nursing. You can go into medicine, intensive care, or a cardiac unit.

When I started, our surgical nursing staff numbered 575 nurses, but this included operating room, surgical intensive care, surgical, and orthopedic departments.

We don't look at surgical patients as being ill. They come in to have something corrected. And most of the people do leave on a pretty good basis, so that can be very satisfying.

DIRECTOR OF MATERNAL-CHILD HEALTH AT A MIDSIZED HOSPITAL

I have been at Norwegian Hospital for eight years. My duties include supervision of obstetrics (OB) and pediatrics. Two units—postpartum and labor and delivery (L&D)—report directly to me. There are twenty-six staff nurses in OB and fifty in labor and delivery. They have no direct unit coordinator over these two units. I'm responsible for them as well as for my other duties as director. I have staff and charge nurses do a lot of things that they would not ordinarily do, such as schedule, quality of care, and improvement issues. They work among themselves to divide up these duties. Postpartum is easier to handle because it's a much smaller group. But in the larger units, such as L&D, there's a mixture of people, part-time to registry. It's more difficult because there are so many more people to get the word out to.

Each shift has an experienced R.N. who's assigned as the charge nurse. These R.N.s give out the assignments and are usually the most experienced persons in the unit. Consequently, they are the resource person for the other staff nurses as to any questions involving patient care, but also in issues having to do with staff. They handle the minor issues but avoid getting involved in anything really serious on a shift-to-shift basis.

Originally I started at the University of Illinois, where I completed two years. After that I left and got married. I got my associate's degree, then completed my master's degree in science and management through National Louis University. I got my associate's degree in 1981, and went right from school to the nursery at Resurrection Hospital in Chicago. My background is in neonatal. I worked for about seven years at Resurrection Hospital before coming to Norwegian.

I came to Norwegian as a part-time staff nurse. At Resurrection they had an agreement with Loyola in which they would transfer their very sick infants to Loyola. I was not able to keep up my skills and it was getting boring. That's when I decided to come to Norwegian, because one of the physicians that I had worked with at Resurrection moved over to Norwegian and said that if I wanted experience, I should go there because Norwegian has a much larger nursery and maternity unit. The population here in Humboldt Park, where Norwegian is located, is a much younger age group. When I first came here we were averaging about four thousand births a year, although in recent years we are averaging fewer—about thirty-six hundred births a year.

We're still up in births compared to other community hospitals—it goes in trends. We have been second in the entire city in the number of births for years. That's why I came here, primarily for the experience. I really like this hospital. The management is very supportive.

One of the things that I like the most is working with the parents. I feel good about helping them through a bad time in their lives, in the cases where the infants are critical. They were expecting a nice chubby little infant and wind up with a scrawny baby—they are even afraid to touch it. I enjoy involving the parents so that they feel comfortable and can trust me and talk to me about their concerns and what their plans will be when they take the baby home. It's a nice exchange. But unfortunately, due to my administrative duties, I am not as closely involved with parents these days, and I really do miss that. Instead I am becoming more supportive of staff in venting their problems or frustrations. I know where they are coming from, having faced these same problems when I was more actively involved in nursing.

You have to be strongly committed to succeed in this field. Today the health care field is very uncertain. You have to be flexible, too, because what you originally intended to do you may be unable to do. For example, if you plan to do hospital nursing, it may be difficult to get into, at least at first. You may have to go a different route, such as public health, to get some experience and then possibly do something like home health before you try for a hospital position. In hospital nursing you are in a more controlled setting. You can always draw upon others for help, but in home health care you are virtually on your own, so you should have a pretty good idea of what you are doing since you won't have the others to support you.

As to training, they are looking for nurses with degrees. But whether or not it's really helpful is a moot point when you are working with staff who have diplomas from hospital schools or associate's degrees from the two-year programs at community colleges. You get lots of hands-on training in both. It's a very intensive program, whereas the bachelor's program gives you a lot more theory. As far as practical experience is concerned, it seems like nurses who come out of diploma or associate's degree programs are more into clinical work; the degree people have all the theory, and this is a little harder to assimilate.

Personally, I look at the individual person more than whether or not he or she has a degree or an associate's degree, so I interview all applicants regardless of academic background.

In a few years you will have to be certified to get into a specialty area, such as intensive care, emergency, pediatrics, surgery, and so forth. The profession also requires that you have continuing education, but no specific amount is stated. It is designed by the individual hospital. Here, for instance, we require that nurses in labor and delivery and nursery be certified in neonatal resuscitation.

Some programs are offered here and others elsewhere. Once certified, you still must be recertified every year and must prove that you are qualified. But it's much easier to be recertified than to get the initial certification. The test is much the same every time you take it.

As for men becoming nurses, we don't see it in maternity or nursery, except for pediatrics. In labor and delivery and postpartum, these are areas where men would not ordinarily be involved. But I have noticed more men involved in areas such as emergency and intensive care.

Opportunities are changing in hospital work. It seems like most hospitals are going through some sort of downsizing. The shifts may be long and require a lot of time and energy. Schedules may require that you work holidays and weekends.

We keep our staff on one shift or the other. You may have to switch between days and evenings occasionally, but you won't have to work nights. But other hospitals may require you to work on the various shifts. We're good to our staff and they tend to stay. We're lucky in that respect.

There are many problems we have to deal with in this area. For instance, in obstetrics, many of our patients are into drugs and have babies that are going through drug withdrawal. This can be very stressful. Also, we occasionally see abused women. This is something you see in the inner-city hospital; it may be true of suburban hospitals, too, but not to the degree that we see. Here, patients are much more open and they will talk about their drug problems. Most of the babies, happily, are not suffering from drug withdrawal problems, but in the eight years that I've been here, it has become much more common.

Part of the problem is that more and more young people are having kids and they are not ready for this responsibility. We need nurses who are supportive and nonjudgmental, nurses who are there to help them.

Yes, the work can be overwhelming at times, but when you see a healthy mother and baby who may have started out very sick, it's rewarding.

To succeed in nursing, you need to be strong in organizational skills and have to be willing to work with the rest of the team. Nursing is very interactive. If you're the kind of person who likes to do your own thing, I don't think that nursing is right for you. You might be better off in research. In nursing you are constantly dealing with people.

I received my bachelor's degree in nursing from the University of Illinois in 1987 and a master's in management from National Louis University in 1996. I was already in nursing before I got my bachelor's because I had completed the two-year associate's degree program at a community college in River Grove.

I started in home health care nursing in 1984, and I worked there for one year before coming to Norwegian Hospital as a staff nurse in 1985. I worked in the special care nursery for premature babies until 1989 and was then promoted to nurse manager of that nursery, where I remained until 1992. I was then promoted to maternity, where I supervised nursing in labor and delivery, nursery, postpartum, and pediatrics.

As Director of Maternal-Child Services, I had about a hundred people reporting to me. In 1994 I was appointed Director of Nurses. As such, I supervise all nursing areas, medical-surgical, pediatrics and maternity, and surgery—emergency and respiratory services.

I always wanted to be a nurse, but had my children first—two sons. In the process of having my kids, I was further exposed to nursing, and I wanted it more than ever. This was a good experience, and I was impressed with nursing as a career at Prentice Women's Hospital at Northwestern University Memorial Hospital.

I enjoy nursing because it involves caring for people when they need a lot of help, helping them to get well so that they can go home, and preventing them from having further health problems. To work in the intensive care nursery, I had to have training in the prenatal intensive area. And I had to be certified in neonatal resuscitation. I went to the University of Illinois intensive care unit for additional training.

When I finished nursing school in 1984, there was an overabundance of nurses. I did not seek out any one specific area, but rather took what was available at the time in a community hospital.

Fortunately, we did not have to deal with death very often. We would deal primarily with premature infants, and sometimes we would encounter congenital defects that were so severe, the child faced death. In those cases, they were transferred to the University of Illinois. Most problems that we had involving death were with respiratory problems. The infants would have to be placed on the respirator so they could breathe.

In maternity it was even more stressful, since you were not just worrying about the infants, but about the mothers as well—you had to handle two patients. In dealing with the mother, you must take into account how this will affect the infant.

Actually there was one infant who was delivered at Norwegian that was very small, less than two pounds at birth. Since the baby was so small, I spent a lot of time with the parents and got to know them quite well. We had to transfer that baby to the University of Illinois, but he was back here after three months, and it was a good feeling that a baby that small was able to go home with his parents. I've stayed in touch with them ever since.

I was a staff nurse in the nursery when the position of Manager of Maternal-Child Nursery opened up. They offered me the job. I thought I would try it, and I have kept going in that direction ever since. When I became Director of Nurses, I went back to school for a management degree.

Staff nurses with a degree earn from $14.50 to $16.00 per hour, and with experience they can get up to $25.00 to $26.00 per hour. The starting level of management in nursing ranges from $24.00 to $28.00 an hour, which translates to about $50,000 to $58,000 per year.

Nursing managers hire the nurses. We are looking for nurses who are committed to the hospital, who will provide excellent quality care, and who are compassionate and professional. Most of the nurses we hire have either their associate's or bachelor's degree. A few have a diploma from a three-year nursing program, but these are rapidly being phased out.

Opportunities seem to go in cycles of seven to ten years. Right now, there are many nurses looking for jobs because of downsizing in hospitals, so we can be more selective in hiring nurses. Although hospital nursing is down, there are more opportunities for nurses in home health care and in HMOs. And the other thing we are seeing is that the patients are so much more ill that the nurses we hire must be very qualified. We also want them to be certified before we hire them.

I prefer working in a smaller community hospital as opposed to working in a big university-affiliated hospital because it has more of a personal family-type setting. Everybody knows everyone else. You don't have to go through a lot of red tape.

In our 220-bed hospital we have about 300 R.N.s and 120 nurse assistants. I hire the managers. We currently have nine. Nurses are professionals and are usually well educated, so in the past we had many levels of managers. We are trying to get away from that now. Our nurses can self-manage. And in the long run, the nurses are the best people to make the decisions.

As to the negatives, there is the possibility of burnout if you are short-staffed. There are times when you can't find enough staff and the nurses may have to work ten to twelve hours a day and take care of too many patients. If this continues for too long, the nurses may start feeling bad about the kind of care they are providing. It's not an easy job; you often have to work long hours and you are on your feet most of the time.

Nurses are involved in professional care and do not become involved with the more common humdrum tasks such as bedpans, making beds, and feeding patients. It's a fulfilling career because you are always helping people, and that gives you a good feeling.

Ordinarily, you would work an eight-hour day, but there are times when you have to work ten to twelve hours a day, even sixteen hours when we are shorthanded. Normally this is not a problem, but in recent weeks we have become very busy because we just became a higher-level emergency room and patients who are quite ill are coming here. We are trying to build up a staff to take care of this problem. During the transition, many nurses have been putting in extra hours and they will be paid accordingly, until we can hire enough nurses to do the job.

In considering a nursing career, you must be the kind of person who can work with people. You must have a lot of patience and physical and mental stamina. You also must be able to deal with stress: for example, if a patient is very sick or in situations where you might have ten admissions at once. You have no way of knowing how many patients will be admitted. You can, for example, staff a unit with three R.N.s and have no patients admitted on one day and then ten admitted the next. So in the latter case, you have to be able to keep cool and know how to organize yourself according to what needs to be done first.

Before getting into nursing, I would tell students to volunteer in a nursing home or hospital to see if they like the work. If they can't deal with stress or get sick to their stomachs when dealing with patients, they need to know this.

There are also opportunities in case management, where you are assigned several cases and follow them all the way through with the goal to get the patient out of the hospital as quickly as possible and to keep costs as low as possible.

The R.N. working in managed care will have to make sure that patients are being cared for in a timely fashion and that their doctors' orders are being followed. Or the hospital itself may be part of an HMO and have its own caseworkers to handle this responsibility.

STAFF NURSE IN A CHILD AND ADOLESCENT PSYCHIATRIC INPATIENT UNIT AT A LARGE MEDICAL TEACHING CENTER

I have been in this unit now for two and a half years, and my title is Clinical Nurse Two. I am enrolled in a master's degree program with the intention of becoming a clinical nurse specialist.

I got my bachelor's degree in nursing in 1994 and a bachelor's in psychology from the University of Dayton in 1992. I am going for my master's of science in nursing with the object of becoming a clinical nurse specialist.

In psychiatry I can order psychological testing for patients, but anything else in tests or in lab work would have to be cosigned by the physician.

Initially, I was interested in going into obstetrics. But once I got into nursing, I found that there were many more options. I began working as a nursing assistant during my clinical experience and I enjoyed it.

I found working with children and adolescent patients very challenging. It's not as technical as medical nursing, but it's demanding. I am still working with children who have suffered physical and substance abuse. It is emotionally challenging work—very hard on the emotions. You need to ask yourself why are you doing this and what are you accomplishing.

Many kids grow up as part of a foster parent system. There is a need to separate your home life from the stresses and problems of your patients, and that is not easy. The idea that you are then helping the patient makes it all worthwhile.

My hours are normal. I am currently working the second shift from 3:00 to 11:00 P.M., and I am married and pregnant with my first child.

I would advise students to take all the science they can in high school— not so much for what they will learn but to develop skills in critical thinking. That has helped me. And it helps if you really love this kind of work. There are many areas of specialization in nursing, but what is needed to succeed is a person with a special aptitude and skill in primary nursing. You will either like this kind of work or you won't.

Some will turn down this field because of the emotional demands that it makes, and others will decline because of the hours or more material considerations. This is quite a departure from most areas of nursing.

You could earn about $35,000 a year, $60,000 with several years of experience. With my master's degree, the opportunities will be even better.

I was not sure what I wanted when I entered nursing, but it was a good choice for me. My background in nursing did not really prepare me for what I am presently doing with psychiatric patients. But through nursing, I did get a better idea of what I could do and in which areas I could specialize.

APPENDIX

A

NURSING ORGANIZATIONS

American Academy of Ambulatory Care Nursing
E. Holly Ave., Box 56
Pitman, NJ 08071-0056
(856) 256-2350

American Academy of Nurse Practitioners
LBJ Building
P.O. Box 12846, Capital Station
Austin, TX 78711
(512) 442-4262

American Academy of Nursing
600 Maryland Ave. NW, Ste. 100 W
Washington, DC 20024-2571
(202) 657-7238

American Assembly for Men in Nursing
43 Twin Bay Dr.
Pensacola, FL 32534-1350

American Association of Neuroscience Nurses
4700 W. Lake St.
Glenview, IL 60025
(847) 375-4733

American Association of Nurse Anesthetists
222 S. Prospect Ave.
Park Ridge, IL 60068-400
(847) 692-7050

American Association of Occupational Health Nurses
2920 Brandywine Rd., Ste. 100
Atlanta, GA 30341
(770) 455-7757

American Association of Office Nurses
109 Kinderkamack Rd.
Montvale, NJ 07645
(201) 391-2600

American Association of Spinal Cord Injury Nurses
75-20 Astoria Blvd.
East Elmhurst, NY 11370-1177
(718) 803-3782

American College of Nurse-Midwives
818 Connecticut Ave. NW, Ste. 900
Washington, DC 20006
(202) 728-9860

American College of Nurse Practitioners
503 Capitol Ct. NE, Ste. 300
Washington, DC 20005
(202) 682-5800

American Licensed Practical Nurses Association
1090 Vermont Ave. NW, Ste. 800
Washington, DC 20005
(202) 682-5800

American Nurses Association
600 Maryland Ave. SW, Ste. 100W
Washington, DC 20024-2571
(202) 651-7000

American Psychiatric Nurses Association
2107 Wilson Blvd., Ste. 300-A
Washington, DC 22201-3042
(703) 242-2443

American Radiological Nurses Association
820 Jorie Blvd.
Oak Brook, IL 60523
(630) 571-9072

American Society of Ophthalmic Registered Nurses
P.O. Box 193030
San Francisco, CA 94119
(415) 561-8513

American Society of Plastic Surgical Nurses
E. Holly Ave., Box 56
Pitman, NJ 08071
(609) 256-2340

Association of Operating Room Nurses
c/o Public Information Coordinator
2170 Parker Rd., Ste. 300
Denver, CO 80231
(303) 755-6300

Association of Rehabilitation Nurses
4700 W. Lake St.
Glenview, IL 60025-1485
(847) 966-3433

Association of Women's Health, Obstetrics, and Neonatal Nurses
2000 L St. NW, Ste. 740
Washington, DC 20036

Dermatology Nurses Association
E. Holly Ave., Box 56
Pitman, NJ 08071
(856) 256-2330

Hospice Nurses Association
Penn Center West 1, Ste. 209
Pittsburgh, PA 15206
(412) 787-9301

National Association of Directors of Nursing
10999 Reed Hartman Hwy., Ste. 233
Cincinnati, OH 45242
(513) 791-3679

National Association of Neonatal Nurses
4700 W. Lake St.
Glenview, IL 60025-1485
(847) 375-3660

National Association of Nurse Practitioners
503 Capitol Ct. NE, Ste. 300
Washington, DC 20002
(202) 543-9693

National Association of Orthopedic Nurses
E. Holly Ave., Box 56
Pitman, NJ 08071-0056
(609) 256-2310

National Association of Pediatric Nurses
1101 Kings Hwy., #206
Cherry Hill, NJ 08034-1912
(609) 667-1773

National Association of Physician Nurses
900 S. Washington St., #G-13
Falls Church, VA 22046
(703) 237-8616

National Association of School Nurses
Lamplighter La.
P.O. Box 1300
Scarborough, ME 04070-1300
(207) 883-2117

National Association of Traveling Nurses
P.O. Box 417-120
Chicago, IL 60641-7120
(708) 453-0080

National League for Nursing
616 Broadway, 33rd Fl.
New York, NY 10006-2701
(212) 363-5555

Oncology Nursing Society
501 Holiday Dr.
Pittsburgh, PA 15220
(412) 921-7373

Respiratory Nursing Society
7794 Grow Dr.
Pensacola, FL 32514
(850) 479-8869

Society of Otorhinolaryngological and Head/Neck Nurses
116 Canal St., Ste. A
New Smyrna Beach, FL 32168
(904) 428-1695

Society of Trauma Nurses
2743 S. Veterans Pkwy.
Springfield, IL 62704
(212) 787-3281

APPENDIX

B

NURSING PUBLICATIONS

American Journal of Nursing
555 W. 57th St.
New York, NY 20019
(212) 582-8820

The Nurse Practitioner
1111 Bethlehem Pike
Box 908
Springhouse, PA 19477
(215) 646-8700

Nurse Week
1156 Alter Dr., Ste. C
Sunnyvale, CA 94086-6801
(408) 249-5877

Nursing & Allied Health Care
National League for Nursing
350 Hudson St.
New York, NY 10019
(212) 989-9392

Nursing Management
1111 Bethlehem Pike
Springhouse, PA 19477
(215) 646-8700

Nursing Opportunities
Medical Economics Publishing Company
5 Paragon Dr.
Montvale, NJ 07645
(201) 358-7200

Nursing Outlook
71830 Westline Industrial Dr.
St. Louis, MO 63146-3318
(314) 872-8370

Nursing Research
American Journal of Nursing Company
555 W. Fifty-Seventh St.
New York, NY 10019
(212) 582-8820

Pediatric Nursing
Janetti Publications, Inc.
E. Holly Dr., Box 56
Pitman, NJ 08071-0056

APPENDIX C

STATE NURSES ASSOCIATIONS

The American Nurses Association (ANA) is a federation of the state nurses associations listed below. In most states, graduating nursing students who join their state nurses association within six months of graduation receive a 50 percent discount on the first year of membership. For additional information on the many benefits available to state nurses association members, call (800) 274-4262 or go to its website at NursingWorld.org.

Alabama State Nurses Association
360 N. Hull St.
Montgomery, AL 36104
(334) 262-8321

Alaska Nurses Association
237 E. Third Ave.
Anchorage, AK 99501
(907) 274-0827

Arizona Nurses Association
1850 E. Southern Ave., Ste. 1
Tempe, AZ 85282
(480) 831-0404

Arkansas Nurses Association
804 N. University
Little Rock, AR 72205
(501) 664-5853

AMA/California
1211 L St., Ste. 501
Sacramento, CA 95814
(916) 447-0225

Colorado Nurses Association
950 S. Cherry St., Ste. 508
Denver, CO 80246
(303) 757-7483

Connecticut Nurses Association
Meritech Business Park
377 Research Pkwy., Ste. 2D
Meriden, CT 06450
(203) 238-1207

Delaware Nurses Association
2644 Capitol Trail, Ste. 330
Newark, DE 19711
(302) 368-2333

District of Columbia Nurses Association
5100 Wisconsin Ave. NW, Ste. 330
Washington, DC 20016
(202) 244-2705

Florida Nurses Association
P.O. Box 536985
Orlando, FL 32853
(407) 896-3261

Georgia Nurses Association
1362 W. Peachtree St. NW
Atlanta, GA 30309
(404) 876-4624

Guam Nurses Association
P.O. Box CG
Hagatna, GU 96932
011 (671) 477-4950/51

Hawaii Nurses Association
677 Ala Moana Blvd., Ste. 301
Honolulu, HI 96813
(808) 531-1628

Idaho Nurses Association
200 N. Fourth St., Ste. 20
Boise, ID 83702
(208) 345-0500

Illinois Nurses Association
105 W. Adams St., Ste. 2101
Chicago, IL 60603
(312) 419-2900

Indiana State Nurses Association
2915 N. High School Rd.
Indianapolis, IN 46224
(317) 299-4575

Iowa Nurses Association
1501 Forty-Second St., Ste. 471
West Des Moines, IA 50266
(515) 225-0495

Kansas State Nurses Association
1208 SW Tyler
Topeka, KS 66612
(785) 233-8638

Kentucky Nurses Association
1400 S. First St.
P.O. Box 2616
Louisville, KY 40201
(502) 637-2546/2547

Louisiana State Nurses Association
5700 Florida Blvd., Ste. 720
Baton Rouge, LA 70806
(225) 201-0971

Maine
Please call ANA membership for information at
(800) 274-4262.

Maryland Nurses Association
849 International Dr.
Airport Square 21, Ste. 255
Linthicum, MD 21090
(410) 859-3000

Massachusetts Association of Registered Nurses
P.O. Box 70668
Quinsigamond Village Station
345 Greenwood St.
Worcester, MA 01607
(800) 274-4262

Michigan Nurses Association
2310 Jolly Oak Rd.
Okemos, MI 48864
(517) 349-5640

Minnesota Nurses Association
1625 Energy Park Dr.
St. Paul, MN 55108
(651) 646-4807

Mississippi Nurses Association
31 Woodgreen Pl.
Madison, MS 39110
(601) 898-0670

Missouri Nurses Association
1904 Bubba La.
P.O. Box 105228
Jefferson City, MO 65110
888-662-MONA (toll free)
(573) 636-4623

Montana Nurses Association
104 Broadway, Ste. G-2
Helena, MT 59601
(406) 442-6710

Nebraska Nurses Association
715 S. Fourteenth St.
Lincoln, NE 68508
(402) 475-3859

Nevada Nurses Association
701 N. Green Valley Pkwy.
Henderson, NV 89014
(702) 260-7886

New Hampshire Nurses Association
48 West St.
Concord, NH 03301
(603) 225-3783

New Jersey State Nurses Association
1479 Pennington Rd.
Trenton, NJ 08618
(609) 883-5335

New Mexico Nurses Association
P.O. Box 80300
Albuquerque, NM 87198
(505) 268-7744

New York State Nurses Association
11 Cornell Rd.
Latham, NY 12110
(518) 782-9400

North Carolina Nurses Association
103 Enterprise St.
P.O. Box 12025
Raleigh, NC 27605
(919) 821-4250

North Dakota Nurses Association
549 Airport Rd.
Bismarck, ND 58504
(701) 223-1385

Ohio Nurses Association
4000 E. Main St.
Columbus, OH 43213
(614) 237-5414

Oklahoma Nurses Association
6414 N. Santa Fe, Ste. A
Oklahoma City, OK 73116
(405) 840-3476

Oregon Nurses Association
9600 SW Oak, Ste. 550
Portland, OR 97223
(503) 293-0011

Pennsylvania State Nurses Association
P.O. Box 68525
Harrisburg, PA 17106
(717) 657-1222

Rhode Island Nurses Association
550 S. Water St., Unit 5408
Providence, RI 02903
(401) 421-9703

South Carolina Nurses Association
1821 Gadsden St.
Columbia, SC 29201
(803) 252-4781

South Dakota Nurses Association
818 E. Forty-First St.
Sioux Falls, SD 57105
(605) 338-1401

Tennessee Nurses Association
545 Mainstream Dr., Ste. 405
Nashville, TN 37228
(615) 254-0350

Texas Nurses Association
7600 Burnet Rd., Ste. 440
Austin, TX 78757
(512) 452-0645

Utah Nurses Association
3761 S 700 E, Ste. 201
Salt Lake City, UT 84106
(801) 293-8351

Vermont Nurses Association
1 Main St., #26 Champlain Mill
Winooski, VT 05404
(802) 655-7123

Virgin Islands State Nurses Association
P.O. Box 583
Christiansted, St. Croix, VI 00821
(809) 773-1261

Virginia Nurses Association
7113 Three Chopt Rd., Ste. 204
Richmond, VA 23226
(804) 282-1808/2373

Washington State Nurses Association
575 Andover Park W, Ste. 101
Seattle, WA 98188
(206) 575-7979

West Virginia Nurses Association
119 Summers St.
Charleston, WV 25301
(304) 342-1169

Wisconsin Nurses Association
6117 Monona Dr.
Madison, WI 53716
(608) 221-0383

Wyoming Nurses Association
Majestic Bldg., Rm. 305
1603 Capitol Ave.
Cheyenne, WY 82001
(307) 635-3955

APPENDIX D

GUIDE TO CERTIFICATION

Here's a list of the certifying boards for various nursing specialties. Information such as titles awarded, requirements for certification, fees, and so forth is also provided.

ADDICTIONS NURSING

Certification Board:
CARN Certification
Center for Education and Testing
801 Paronia Ave., Ste. 201
Jersey City, NJ 07306
Title Awarded: CARN

Requirements: Must have three years of experience practicing as an R.N. and four thousand hours of addictions nursing practice as an R.N. within the past five years. Experience may be as a staff nurse, administrator, educator, consultant, counselor, private practitioner, or researcher.

Fees: NNSA members, $175; nonmembers, $260. Valid for four years; may retake exam or document continuing education.

CHILDBIRTH EDUCATORS

Certification Board:
ASPO/Lamaze
1200 Nineteenth St. NW, Ste. 300
Washington, DC 20036
Title Awarded: LCCE

Requirements: Must be a graduate of a Lamaze-accredited childbirth educator program; or a currently licensed R.N., C.N.M., R.P.T., M.D.; or awarded a baccalaureate or higher degree from a recognized institute of higher education; or a graduate of another childbirth educator program (for example, ICEA, Bradley, Best). You will also need documentation of three years of childbirth education teaching experience within the past five years, consisting of at least 144 instructional hours; and documentation of 30 contact hours of continuing education applicable to childbirth education within the past three years.

Fees: Lamaze International members, $225; nonmembers, $350.

CRITICAL CARE NURSING

Certification Board:
AACN Certification Corporation
101 Columbia
Aliso Viejo, CA 92656

Fees: AACN members, $150; nonmembers, $225.

Certification Board:
Adult Critical-Care Nursing
Title Awarded: CCRN

Requirements: Must have one year of experience in adult critical care nursing practice within the past two years (1,750 hours) with 875 hours in the year previous to application. Current unrestricted R.N. license in the United States.

Certification Board:
Neonatal Critical-Care Nursing
Title Awarded: CCRN

Requirements: Must have one year of experience in neonatal critical care nursing practice within the past two years (1,750 hours) with 875 hours in the year previous to application. Current unrestricted R.N. license in the United States.

Certification Board:
Pediatric Critical-Care Nursing
Title Awarded: CCRN
Requirements: Must have one year of experience in pediatric critical care nursing practice within the past two years (1,750 hours) with 875 hours in the year previous to application. Current unrestricted R.N. license in the United States.

DIABETES EDUCATORS

Certification Board:
National Certification Board for Diabetes Educators
330 E. Algonquin Rd., Ste. 4
Arlington Heights, IL 60005
Title Awarded: CDE
Requirements: Multidisciplinary. Must hold unrestricted U.S. license or registration as an R.N., R.D., physician, pharmacist, podiatrist, P.A., P.T., O.T., or be a health care professional with a minimum of a master's degree from an accredited U.S. college or university in: nutrition, social work, clinical psychology, exercise physiology, health education, or specified concentrations in public health. Must be currently practicing in diabetes patient and self-management education within the United States or its territories. Must have completed a minimum of two years of experience as a diabetes educator and a minimum of one thousand hours of professional practice experience in diabetes patient and self-management education within the United States or its territories over a period of no fewer than two years and no more than five years after meeting education requirements, and before applying for the certification exam. Fees: $250. Valid for 5 years; must retake the exam.

EMERGENCY NURSING

Certification Board:
Board of Certification for Emergency Nursing
915 Lee St.
Des Plaines, IL 60016

    Requirements: Must have current unrestricted license as an RN. Recommended: two years of experience in emergency nursing practice. Valid for four years.

Certification Board:
Flight Nursing
Title Awarded: CFRN

    Requirements: Must have current unrestricted R.N. license. Recommended: two years of experience in flight nursing practice. Valid for four years.

GASTROENTEROLOGY

Certification Board:
Certifying Board of Gastroenterology Nurses and Associates, Inc.
3525 N. Ellicott Mills Dr., Ste. N
Ellicott City, MD 21043
Title Awarded: CGN, CGRN

    Requirements: Must have worked in gastroenterology for two years fulltime or its part-time equivalent within the past five years; or four thousand hours.

    Fees: SGNA (Society of Gastroenterology Nurses and Associates) members, $300; nonmembers, $350. Valid for five years; must retake the exam or recertify by contact hours (100).

HEALTH CARE QUALITY

Certification Board:
Health Care Quality Certification Board

P.O. Box 1880

San Gabriel, CA 91778

cphq.org

Title Awarded: CPHQ

Requirements: Interdisciplinary for R.N.s, medical records technologists, physicians, other clinicians, and managers. Must have a minimum of an associate's degree. Alternate eligibility preapplication review is available. Must have practiced two years in health care quality, case, utilization, and/or risk-management activities within the last five years by date of exam.

Fees: NAHO members, $235; nonmembers, $300.

Recertification: 30 CE hours every two years. Valid for two years.

HIV/AIDS NURSING

Certification Board:

HIV/AIDS Nursing Certification Board

c/o Professional Testing Corporation

1350 Broadway

New York, NY 10018

Title Awarded: AIDS Certified Registered Nurse (ACRN)

Requirements: Must hold current license as R.N. in the United States, or international equivalent, and have two years of experience in clinical practice, education, management, or research in HIV/AIDS nursing. Valid for four years.

Recertification: Retake the exam or acquire forty CEUs.

Fees: ANAC members, $200; nonmembers: $350.

HOLISTIC NURSING

Certification Board:

American Holistic Nurses Certification Corp.

5102 Ganymede Dr.

Austin, TX 78727

Title Awarded: HNC

Requirements: Must have current unrestricted license as an R.N. (minimum of a baccalaureate). Minimum of one year full-time practice as a holistic nurse or part-time for a minimum of two thousand hours within last five years. Minimum of 48 current hours of continuing education in areas of holistic nursing. Must meet criteria for qualitative assessment and pass the national exam. Call (877) 284-0998 for information.

Fees: $25 application; $150 qualitative assessment; $210 quantitative test. Valid for five years.

Recertification: 100 CE hours, of which 20 must be in holistic nursing.

HOSPICE AND PALLIATIVE NURSING

Certification Board:
National Board for Certification of Hospice and Palliative Nurses
Medical Center East, Ste. 375
211 N. Whitfield St.
Pittsburgh, PA 15206-3031
Title Awarded: CHPN

Requirements: Must be currently licensed as an R.N. in the United States or the equivalent in Canada; at least two years of experience in hospice and palliative nursing practice recommended.

Fees: HPNA members, $230; nonmembers, $330; renewal: members, $195; nonmembers, $295.

INFECTION CONTROL

Certification Board:
Certification Board of Infection Control and Epidemiology, Inc.
4700 W. Lake Ave.
Glenview, IL 60025-1485
cbic.org
Title Awarded: CIC

Requirements: Interdisciplinary; for R.N.s, medical technologists, and physicians. Candidate must have a minimum of a baccalaureate in a health care–related field. There is a waiver process for candidates who do not meet the education requirements. Must have practiced infection control for a minimum of 2 years.

Fees: $245; recertification, $195. Valid for five years; may retake the exam or the Self-Assessment Recertification Examination (SARE).

INTRAVENOUS NURSING

Certification Board:
Intravenous Nurses Certification Corporation
10 Fawcett St.
Cambridge, MA 02138
Title Awarded: CRNI

Requirements: Minimum of 1,600 hours of experience as an R.N. in intravenous therapy within last two years prior to date of application. Candidate must have active current license in the United States or Canada and must complete the CRNI examination registration form.

Fees: INS members, $250; nonmembers, $400.

Recertification: $100. Every three years by exam or by continuing education.

LACTATION CONSULTANT

Certification Board:
International Board of Lactation Consultant Examiners
7309 Arlington Blvd., Ste. 300
Falls Church, VA 22042
Title Awarded: IBCLC

Requirements: Must have 30 hours of continuing education related to breast-feeding within three years prior to taking the exam. Those with a baccalaureate or higher must have 2,500 BC practice hours; those with 60 academic credits (associate's degree or R.N. diploma) must have four thousand hours of practice. Alternate pathways are available.

Fee: $395. Valid for five years.

Recertification: By exam or by continuing education; every ten years by exam only.

LEGAL NURSE CONSULTING

Certification Board:
American Legal Nurse Consultant Certification Board
4700 W. Lake Ave.
Glenview, IL 60025-1485
aalnc.org
Title Awarded: LNCC

Requirements: Must possess a full and unrestricted license as an R.N. in the United States or its territories; have a bachelor's degree or the equivalent of five years of experience as a legal nurse consultant (beginning in 2004, applicants must have a B.S.N.); have practiced two years as an R.N.; have evidence of two thousand hours of legal nurse consulting experience in a staff, administrative, teaching, or private practice capacity within the three years prior to the application.

Fees: AALNC members, $250; nonmembers, $350. Valid for five years; may retake the exam or CE credits.

NEPHROLOGY NURSING

Certification Board:
Board of Nephrology Examiners Nursing and Technology (BONENT)
P.O. Box 15945-282
Titles Awarded:
Hemodialysis—CHN
Peritoneal dialysis—CPDN
Hemodialysis technology—CHT

Requirements: Must have current U.S. license; technologists must have high school diploma or equivalent; both must have one year's experience in caring for patients with end-stage renal disease.

Fees: Exam, $195; annual fee, $50.

Recertification: Every four years, must submit documentation of 45 CEUs (30 nephrology-related) every four years or retake exam.

Certification Board:
Nephrology Nursing Certification Board

East Holly Ave., Box 56

Pitman, NJ 08071-0056

Title Awarded: CNN

Requirements: Must possess a B.S.N.; hold a current unrestricted license as a registered nurse in the United States and its territories. Within three years prior to application, must have a minimum of two years of nephrology experience as an R.N. in general staff, administrative, teaching, or research with at least 50 percent of employment hours in nephrology nursing; and complete 30 CEUs for fundamental nephrology nursing.

Fees: ANNA members, $175; nonmembers, $225. Certification valid for three years.

Recertification: By accruing 60 CE contact hours during that period, or retake the test.

NEUROSCIENCE NURSING

Certification Board:

American Board of Neuroscience Nursing

4700 W. Lake Ave.

Glenview, IL 60025

Title Awarded: CNRN

Requirements: Must have two years of experience in neuroscience nursing. Must be engaged in clinical practice or as a consultant, researcher, administrator, or educator in neuroscience nursing.

Fees: AANN members, $215; nonmembers, $300. Valid five years.

Recertification: Through CE units or retake the exam.

NURSE ADMINISTRATION—LONG-TERM CARE

Certification Board:

NADONA/LTC Certification Registrar

10999 Reed Hartman Hwy., Ste. 223

Cincinnati, OH 45242-8301

Title Awarded: CDONA/LTC

Requirements: Must be director of nursing administration in long-term care setting for at least 12 months in five years. Former DONs and assistant DONs are eligible to take the exam.

Fees: NADONA/LTC members, $125; nonmembers, $200. Valid for five years.

Recertification: $60 fee and validation of 75 hours of continuing education every five years.

NURSE ANESTHETISTS

Certification Board:
Council on Certification of Nurse Anesthetists*
222 S. Prospect Ave.
Park Ridge, IL 60068-5790
Title Awarded: CRNA

Requirements: Must be a graduate of a nurse anesthesia educational program accredited by the Council on Accreditation of Nurse Anesthesia Educational Programs and maintain a current unrestricted R.N. license in the United States and its territories. Must certify that an R.N. license is not currently under and has not been subject to investigation or legal action, and that individual has no mental, physical, or other problems that could interfere with the practice of anesthesia.

Fee: $550.

Recertification: Every two years; document 40 hours of approved continuing education, current licensure as R.N., engaged in anesthesia practice; no mental, physical, or other problems that could interfere with the practice of anesthesia.

NURSE MIDWIFERY

Certification Board:
ACNM Certification Council, Inc.
8401 Corporate Dr., Ste. 630
Landover, MD 20785
Title Awarded: CNM/CM

Requirements: Satisfactory completion of a nurse-midwifery program accredited by ACNM. Exam must be taken within 12 months of completing the program.

Recertification: Every eight years by (option 1) completing three ACC certificate maintenance modules (antepartum, intrapartum/newborn and postpartum/gynecology,) and accruing two CEUs of ACNM or ACCME Category 1–approved activities; or (option 2) passing exam and accruing two CEUs of ACNM or ACCME Category 1–approved activities.

Fee: $425 for initial exam; $55 per year for certificate maintenance.

OCCUPATIONAL HEALTH NURSING

Certification Board:

American Board for Occupational Health Nurses, Inc.

201 E. Ogden, Ste. 114

Hinsdale, IL 60521-3652

Title Awarded: COHN, COHN-S†

Requirements: Must prove 50 course contact hours in occupational health or in courses related to occupational health, taken within the preceding five years; have two years (four thousand hours) of experience in occupational health nursing; have valid nursing license; and be employed a minimum of eight hours a week in occupational health nursing. Individual consideration is given to occupational health nurses who meet the experience criteria but are currently enrolled full-time in a graduate program of study in occupational health nursing or in a related field. For COHN-S, a baccalaureate in nursing is required.

Fees: application: $50; exam, $275; recertification, $225. Valid for five years.

Recertification: 75 CE hours in occupational health and four thousand hours of work experience or 100 CE hours and three thousand hours of work experience.

Certification Board:

Occupational Health Nurse Care Manager

Title Awarded: COHN/CM, COHN-S/CM

Requirements: Must have current COHN or COHN-S, current nursing license, and 10 CE hours in case management in past five years.

Fees: application, $35; exam, $150; recertification, $100. Valid for five years.

Recertification: 10 CE hours in occupational health, case management, and continued base certification.

ONCOLOGY NURSING

Certification Board:
Oncology Nursing Certification Corporation*
501 Holiday Dr.
Pittsburgh, PA 15220-2749
Title Awarded: OCN

Requirements: Must have a minimum of 12 months of experience as an R.N. within the last three years, 1,000 hours of oncology nursing practice within the last 30 months, and current R.N. license.

Fees: ONS members, $195; nonmembers, $285. Valid for four years; may renew every other cycle by ONC-PRO; must take test at least every eight years.

Recertification: ONS members, $150; nonmembers, $240.

Title Awarded: AOCN

Requirements: Must have minimum of 30 months of experience as an R.N. within the five years prior to application, two thousand hours of oncology nursing practice within the past five years, current R.N. license, and master's degree or higher in nursing.

Fees: ONS members, $225; nonmembers, $315. Valid for four years; may renew every other cycle by ONC-PRO; must take test at least every eight years.

Recertification: ONS members, $180; nonmembers, $270.

OPHTHALMIC NURSING

Certification Board:
National Certifying Board for Ophthalmic Registered Nurses
P.O. Box 193030

San Francisco, CA 94119

Title Awarded: CRNO

Requirements: Must have at least two years of full-time (four thousand hours) experience in ophthalmic nursing practice.

Fees: ASORN members, $225; nonmembers, $300. Valid for five years; must retake the exam.

ORTHOPAEDIC NURSING

Certification Board:

Orthopaedic Nurses Certification Board*

East Holly Ave., Box 56

Pitman, NJ 08071

Title Awarded: ONC

Requirements: Must have two years of experience practicing as an R.N. holding a current and unrestricted license, and 1,000 hours of work experience in orthopaedic nursing practice within the past three years.

Fees: NAON members, $205; nonmembers, $285. Valid for five years, may retake the exam or document 100 continuing education hours.

PAIN MANAGEMENT

Certification Board:

American Academy of Pain Management

13947 Mono Way #A

Sonora, CA 95370

Title Awarded: FAAPM

Requirements: Interdisciplinary with three levels of certification. Nurses who are doctorally prepared earn a diplomate status; nurses with a master's degree earn a fellowship. Both must have two years of experience working with patients who have pain. Baccalaureate-prepared nurses earn clinical associate status and must have five years of relevant experience in pain management. All must submit three professional letters of reference, official academic transcripts, curriculum vitae, license, and application. Must also pass the certification exam.

Fee: $250 (general membership, $150; application, $100); exam, $175; annual renewal fee, $150. Valid for four years.

Recertification: By documenting 100 contact hours of continuing education.

PEDIATRIC NURSING

Certification Board:
National Certification Board of Pediatric Nurse Practitioners and Nurses
800 S. Frederick Ave., Ste. 104
Gaithersburg, MD 20877-41150
General Pediatric Nursing
Title Awarded: CPN

Requirements: Must provide documentation of current R.N. licensure in the United States and completion of basic R.N. education (diploma, associate's, baccalaureate, or master's degree). Must document two years of full-time or equivalent experience (total 3,600 hours minimum) as an R.N. in a pediatric nursing specialty in a U.S. facility within the past four years, including direct patient care, teaching, administration, clinical research, or consultation in pediatric nursing.

Fees: $260. Valid for five years; renewed annually by documentation of 10 CEUs or one academic credit in pediatric nursing, or re-examination within five years of certification. All exams are computer-based, given year-round through Prometric/Sylvan Technology Testing Centers.

Certification Board:
Pediatric Nurse Practitioner
Title Awarded: CPNP

Requirements: Must be a graduate of a PNP master's, post-master's, or doctoral program recognized by NCBPNP/N, and submit documentation including transcripts showing degrees conferred. Must pass exam within 24 months after completing program. An alternative pathway and certification by endorsement are also offered.

Fee: $375. Annual certification maintenance through self-assessment exercise, 10 CEUs/year, and/or documentation of clinical PNP practice. All exams are computer-based, given year-round through Prometric/Sylvan Technology Testing Centers.

PEDIATRIC ONCOLOGY

Certification Board:

Oncology Nursing Certification Corporation

501 Holiday Dr.

Pittsburgh, PA 15220-2749

oncc.org

Title Awarded: CPON

Requirements: Must have minimum of 12 months' experience as an R.N., 1,000 hours pediatric oncology nursing practice within the past 30 months, and current R.N. license.

Fees: ONS and APON members, $225; nonmembers, $315. Valid for four years.

Recertification: Members, $180; nonmembers, $270. After passing ONCC-administered CPON exam, may renew every other year by ONC-PRO. Must retake test every eight years.

PERIANESTHESIA NURSING

Certification Board:

The American Board of Perianesthesia Nursing Certification, Inc.

475 Riverside Dr., 7th Fl.

New York, NY 10115-0089

cpancapa.org

Title Awarded: CPAN, CAPA

Requirements: Candidates applying for CPAN or CAPA certification must hold a current unrestricted R.N. license and have a minimum of 1,800 hours of direct perianesthesia practice experience as an R.N. during the past three consecutive years. Nurses working as direct caregiver, manager, teacher, or researcher in perianesthesia are eligible for certification. Candidates may contact ABPANC's national office to inquire which certification exam would be appropriate for them.

Fees: ASPAN member, $235; nonmember, $335.

Recertification: Member, $150; nonmember, $280. Certification valid for three years; recertification by examination or continuing learning program.

PERIOPERATIVE NURSING

Certification Board:
National Certification Board of Perioperative Nursing
2170 S. Parker Rd., Ste. 295
Denver, CO 80231-5710
Title Awarded: CNOR

Requirements: Must have a minimum of two full years and 2,400 hours of operating room practice as an R.N., employed within the previous two years, either full-time or part-time as an R.N. in an administrative, teaching, research, or general staff capacity in perioperative nursing.

Fees: $250 for AORN members; 350 for nonmembers. Valid for five years; may retake the exam or document 150 contact hours of approved continuing education.

Certification Board:
R.N. First Assistant Role
Title Awarded: CRNFA

Requirements: Must be certified as a CNOR; must document two thousand hours of practice in the R.N. first assistant role, with at least five hundred hours in the past two years; must have attended a formal RNFA program; must be B.S.N. prepared.

Fee: $375 for AORN members; $500 for nonmembers. Valid for five years; must retest or submit continuing education to recertify.

PLASTIC AND RECONSTRUCTIVE SURGICAL NURSING

Certification Board:
Plastic Surgical Nursing Certification Board
East Holly Ave., P.O. Box 56
Pitman, NJ 08071
Title Awarded: CPSN

Requirements: Must have a minimum of two years of experience in plastic surgical nursing as an R.N. in a general staff, administrative, teaching, or research capacity within five years prior to application, and have spent at least 50 percent of practice hours in plastic surgical nursing during two of the preceding five years.

Fees: ASPRSN members, $175; nonmembers, $275. Valid for three years; may retake the exam or obtain 45 contact hours of continuing education with a minimum of 30 in plastic surgical nursing.

Recertification: ASPRSN members, $100; nonmembers, $175.

REHABILITATION NURSING

Certification Board:
Rehabilitation Nursing Certification Board*
4700 W. Lake Ave.
Glenview, IL 60025-1485
Title Awarded: CRRN

Requirements: Must have current, unrestricted R.N. license and education in rehabilitation nursing; minimum of two years of practice as an R.N. in rehabilitation nursing in the last five years (may include supervision of others to achieve patient goals or one year of experience as an R.N. in rehabilitation nursing and one year of advanced study (beyond baccalaureate) in nursing. Rehabilitation nursing experience must be verified by two professional colleagues, one of whom is a CRRN or immediate supervisor.

Fees: ARN members, $195; nonmembers, $285. Valid for five years; retake the exam or recertify by 60 points of credit with a combination of continuing education, presentations, professional publications, formal course work, and/or submitting test items.

Title Awarded: CRRN-A

Requirements: Must be CRRN with an unrestricted nursing license and master's degree in nursing or doctorate in nursing.

Fees: ARN members, $230; nonmembers, $310. Valid 5 years.

SCHOOL NURSING

Certification Board:
National Board for Certification of School Nurses, Inc.
P.O. Box 1300
Scarborough, ME 04070-1300
Title Awarded: CSN

Requirements: Must be currently licensed as an R.N. with a baccalaureate degree. Three years of experience as a school nurse is recommended.

Fees: NASN members, $175; nonmembers, $250.

UROLOGY NURSING

Certification Board:

American Board of Urologic Allied Health Professionals, Inc.

East Holly Ave., P.O. Box 56

Pitman, NJ 08071-0056

Titles Awarded: CURN, CUA, CUNP, CUCNS, CUPA

Requirements: R.N., L.P.N., L.V.N., P.A.: current licensure and one year of experience in urology nursing practice. Other associates: three years of in-service training under supervision of a practicing urologist. Advanced practice: same as R.N., but with current recognition by state board of nursing as nurse practitioner and/or clinical nurse specialist, and an earned master's degree in nursing.

Fees: SUNA members, $195; nonmembers, $255; advanced practice SUNA members, $225; nonmembers, $285. Valid for three years; may either retest or provide proof of 50 contact hours.

WOMEN'S HEALTH NURSING

Certification Board:

National Certification Corporation for the Obstetric, Gynecologic, and Neonatal Nursing Specialties

P.O. Box 11082

Chicago, IL 60611-0082

nccnet.org

Requirements: For all categories, must have experience/employment in direct patient care, education, administration, and/or research. Written exam given four times a year; valid for three years. Certification Maintenance Program requires 45 contact hours of approved CE or reexamination for RNC, and 15 hours approved CE or reexam for subspecialty.

Breast-Feeding

Requirements: Must pass subspecialty exam; be licensed R.N. in the United States or Canada; be employed. Pathway 1: Must be certified by NCC, ACNM, or ANCC. Pathway 2: Must have 24 months of practice in the specialty.

Fees: NCC RNCs, $100; non-NCC RNCs, $135.

Electronic Fetal Monitoring

Requirements: Must pass subspecialty exam; be licensed R.N., M.D., or physician's assistant in the United States or Canada.

Fees: NCC RNCs, $100; non-NCC RNCs, $135.

Inpatient Obstetric Nurse

Requirements: For the following specialties, must be a licensed R.N. in the United States or Canada and have 24 months of experience in the specialty, including a minimum of two thousand hours as an R.N. Employment within the last 24 months is required.

Fee: $250

Low-Risk Neonatal Nurse
Maternal Newborn Nurse
Neonatal Intensive Care Nurse
Neonatal Nurse Practitioner

Requirements: Must be a licensed R.N. in the United States or Canada; a graduate of a master's or post-master's degree neonatal nurse practitioner program at least one academic year in length and acceptable to NCC; and have two hundred didactic hours and six hundred clinical hours.

Primary Care Nurse Practitioner–Obstetrics

Requirements: Must be a licensed R.N. in the United States or Canada; be certified by ANCC, AANP, or NCBPNP. Current employment required.

Fee: $135

Primary Care Nurse Practitioner–Gynecology/Reproductive Health Care

Requirements: Must be a licensed R.N. in the United States or Canada; be certified by ANCC, AANP, or NCBPNP. Current employment is required.

Fee: $135

Women's Health Care Nurse Practitioner

Title Awarded: RNC

Requirements: Must be licensed R.N. in the United States or Canada; a graduate of a women's health care nurse practitioner program that is at least one academic year in length and is acceptable to NCC; and have two hundred didactic hours and six hundred clinical hours. Effective January 1, 2007, a graduate degree will be required.

CERTIFICATES AWARDED BY THE AMERICAN NURSES CREDENTIALING CENTER

Certification Board:

600 Maryland Ave. SW, Ste. 100 W

Washington, DC 20024-2571

Requirements: All candidates must hold a currently active R.N. license.

Fees: ANA members, $156; nonmembers, $296; discount, $226.

Acute Care Nurse Practitioner

Title Awarded: CS

Requirements: Must hold a master's or higher degree in nursing. Must have been prepared in an acute care nurse practitioner master's degree program, or a formal postgraduate acute case nurse practitioner program within a school of nursing granting graduate-level academic credit; or an adult nurse practitioner master's degree in nursing program with a minimum of five hundred hours of post-master's practice within two years after completion of the ANP program in an advanced practice role, providing direct services to patients who are acutely or critically ill.

Adult Nurse Practitioner*

Title Awarded: CS

Requirements: Must hold a master's or higher degree in nursing. Must have been prepared as an adult nurse practitioner (ANP) in either an ANP master's degree in nursing program or a family nurse practitioner master's degree in nursing program; or in a formal postgraduate ANP or family nurse practitioner track or program within a school of nursing granting graduate-level academic credit.

Cardiac Rehabilitation Nurse*

Title Awarded: C

Requirements: Must hold a baccalaureate or higher degree in nursing. Must have practiced as a licensed R.N. for a minimum of two years; provide evidence of successful completion of American Heart Association ACLS program; currently practice in a cardiac rehabilitation setting an average of eight hours per week; have a minimum of two thousand hours of hospital experience either in critical care or acute coronary care; have 30 contact hours of continuing education applicable to cardiac rehabilitation within the past three years.

Case Management (Exam 30)

(Modular Certification)

Title Awarded: Cm

Requirements: Must have a core nursing specialty certification. Must hold a baccalaureate or higher degree in nursing; have functioned within the scope of an R.N. case manager a minimum of two thousand hours within the past two years.

Case Management (Exam 31)

(Modular Certification)

Title Awarded: Cm

Requirements: For candidates who do not hold a core nursing specialty certification. Must hold a baccalaureate or higher degree in nursing; have functioned as an R.N. for four thousand hours, with at least two thousand of those hours as a nurse case manager within the past two years.

Clinical Specialist in Adult Psychiatric Mental Health Nursing*
Clinical Specialist in Child and Adolescent Psychiatric and
Mental Health Nursing*

Title Awarded: CS

Requirements: Must hold a master's or higher degree in nursing with a university-identified major in psychiatric and mental health (PMH) nursing; or hold a master's or higher degree in nursing outside the PMH field with a minimum of 18 graduate or postgraduate academic credits in PMH theory. A minimum of nine of these 18 graduate or postgraduate credits must contain didactic and clinical experiences specific to PMH nursing theory. Must be currently involved in direct patient contact an average of four hours per week. Must be currently involved in clinical consultation or supervision and have experience in at least two different treatment modalities. Must have eight hundred hours of direct patient/client contact in advanced clinical practice of PMH nursing; up to four hundred of these hours may be earned through the clinical practicum of the master's program. Must document 100 hours of supervision with a qualified supervisor. Up to 50 hours of supervision may be earned within the master's program.

Clinical Specialist in Community Health Nursing*

Title Awarded: CS

Requirements: Must hold a master's or higher degree in nursing with a specialization in community/public health nursing; currently practice an average of 12 hours weekly in community/public health nursing; have practiced post-master's a minimum of eight hundred hours in community/public health nursing in the past 24 months. Applications will also be reviewed with a master's or higher degree in nursing or a baccalaureate in nursing and a master's or higher degree in public health.

Clinical Specialist in Gerontological Nursing*

Title Awarded: CS

Requirements: Must hold a master's or higher degree in gerontological nursing, or with a specialization in gerontological nursing. Must have practiced 12 months following completion of the master's degree. If a clinical specialist, must have provided eight hundred hours (post-master's) of direct patient care or clinical management in gerontological nursing in the past 24 months. If a consultant, researcher, educator, or administrator, must have provided four hundred hours (post-master's) of direct patient care or clinical management in gerontological nursing in the past 24 months.

Clinical Specialist in Home Health Nursing

Title Awarded: CS

Requirements: Must hold a master's or higher degree in nursing and within the past 24 months have practiced as a licensed R.N. in Home Health Nursing a minimum of 1,000 hours (post-master's). If graduated from a CS in Home Health Nursing program, 50 percent of the clinical practice within the graduate program may be applied toward the 1,000-hour practice requirement. Must currently provide at least eight hours per week of direct patient care or clinical management in home health nursing.

Clinical Specialist in Medical-Surgical Nursing*

Title Awarded: CS

Requirements: Must hold a master's degree in nursing with evidence of medical-surgical concentration; be currently providing direct patient care in medical-surgical nursing an average of four hours or more weekly; have practiced 12 months following completion of the master's degree; have provided 800 hours of direct patient care within the past 24 months. If employed as a consultant, researcher, administrator, or educator, must have provided direct patient care in medical-surgical nursing four hundred hours (post-master's) within the past 24 months.

College Health Nurse*

Title Awarded: C

Requirements: Must hold a baccalaureate or higher degree in nursing; have a minimum of 1,500 hours of practice as a licensed R.N. in college health nursing; and currently practice college health nursing an average of eight hours per week (a minimum of 288 hours per year). Must have 30 contact hours of continuing education in specialty in past three years.

Community Health Nurse*

Title Awarded: C

Requirements: Must hold a baccalaureate or higher degree in nursing; have practiced as a licensed R.N. in community health nursing a minimum of 1,500 hours; have 30 contact hours of continuing education in the specialty in the past three years.

Family Nurse Practitioner*

Title Awarded: CS

Requirements: Must hold a master's or higher degree in nursing; have been prepared as a family nurse practitioner (FNP) in either an FNP master's degree in nursing program, or a formal postgraduate FNP track or program within a school of nursing granting graduate-level academic credit.

General Nursing Practice

Title Awarded: C

Requirements: Must have a baccalaureate or higher degree in nursing. Must have a minimum of four thousand hours as an R.N. in general nursing practice, two thousand of which were within the past three years. This requirement can be met by providing direct patient care or clinical management, or supervision, education, or direction of others to achieve patient goals.

Gerontological Nurse*

Title Awarded: C

Requirements: Must hold a baccalaureate or higher degree in nursing. Must have a minimum of four thousand hours of practice as an R.N. in gerontological nursing, two thousand of which must have been within the past two years. (Time spent in a formal program of advanced nursing study may count toward three hundred hours.) Must have had 30 contact hours of continuing education applicable to gerontology/gerontological nursing within the past two years. Requirements can be met if engaged in direct patient care or clinical management or in supervision, education, or direction of others to achieve patient goals.

Gerontological Nurse Practitioner*

Title Awarded: CS

Requirements: Must hold a master's degree in nursing. Must have been prepared as a nurse practitioner in either a gerontological nurse practitioner (GNP) master's degree in nursing program or a formal postgraduate GNP track or program within a school of nursing that is currently granting graduate-level academic credit.

Home Health Nurse*

Title Awarded: C

Requirements: Must hold an active R.N. license; hold a baccalaureate or higher degree in nursing; have practiced as a licensed R.N. in home health nursing a minimum of 1,500 hours; currently practice home health nursing a minimum of eight hours per week; have 20 contact hours of continuing education in specialty within the past two years.

Informatics Nurse

Title Awarded: C

Requirements: Must hold a baccalaureate or higher degree in nursing; have practiced as a licensed R.N. for a minimum of two years; have practiced at least two thousand hours in the field of informatics nursing within the past five years or have completed at least 12 semester hours of credits in informatics in a graduate program in nursing and have practiced a minimum of 1,000 hours within the past five years; have 20 contact hours of continuing education in specialty in the past two years.

Medical-Surgical Nurse*

Title Awarded: C

Requirements: Must hold a baccalaureate or higher degree in nursing. Must have practiced as an R.N. a minimum of four thousand hours in medical-surgical nursing, with two thousand hours being within the past two years, and currently practice medical-surgical nursing an average of eight hours per week. Requirements may be met if engaged in direct patient care or clinical management or in supervision, education, or direction of others to achieve patient goals. Also must have 30 contact hours of continuing education in specialty within past three years.

Nursing Administration*

Title Awarded: CNA

Requirements: Must hold a baccalaureate or higher degree in nursing. Must have held an administrative position at the nurse manager or nurse executive level for at least 24 months of full-time service within the past five years. Must have 30 contact hours of continuing education in specialty in the past two years or hold a master's degree in nursing.

Nursing Administration, Advanced*

Title Awarded: CNAA

Requirements: Must hold a master's or higher degree. For nurses first licensed in 1990 and after, if the master's degree is not in nursing, a baccalaureate in nursing will be required. Also must have held an administrative position at the nurse executive level for at least 24 months of full-time service within the past five years. Must have 30 contact hours of continuing education in specialty in the past two years or hold a master's degree in nursing administration.

Nursing Continuing Education/Staff Development*

Title Awarded: C

Requirements: Must hold a baccalaureate or higher degree in nursing; have practiced as an R.N. in nursing continuing education and/or staff development for a minimum of four thousand hours during the past five years; currently practice as a licensed R.N. in nursing continuing education and/or staff development an average of 20 hours or more per week. Must have 20 contact hours of continuing education in specialty in past two years.

Pediatric Nurse*

Title Awarded: C

Requirements: Must hold a baccalaureate or higher degree in nursing. Must have at least 2,100 hours as an R.N. in pediatric nursing in direct patient care or clinical management, supervision, education, or the direction of others to achieve patient goals. Also must have 30 contact hours of continuing education applicable to pediatric nursing within the past three years.

Pediatric Nurse Practitioner*

Title Awarded: CS

Requirements: Must have been prepared as a nurse practitioner in a pediatric nurse practitioner (PNP) master's degree program or a formal postgraduate PNP track or program within a school of nursing granting graduate-level academic credit. Must have practiced as a PNP for six hundred hours within the past three years.

Perinatal Nurse*

Title Awarded: C

Requirements: Must hold a baccalaureate or higher degree in nursing. Must have practiced 2,100 hours as an R.N. in perinatal nursing in the past three years. (Time spent in a formal program of advanced nursing study may count for three hundred hours.) Also must have had 30 contact hours of continuing education in specialty within the past three years.

Psychiatric and Mental Health Nurse*

Title Awarded: C

Requirements: Must hold a baccalaureate or higher degree in nursing. Must have practiced as an R.N. in direct psychiatric and mental health nursing 24 of the past 48 months. Within this time, must have engaged in direct psychiatric and mental health nursing a minimum of 1,600 hours; be currently involved in direct psychiatric and mental health nursing practice for an average of eight hours per week; have access to clinical consultation/supervision; and provide a reference from a nurse colleague. Must also have 30 contact hours of continuing education applicable to specialty area within the past three years.

School Nurse

Title Awarded: C

Requirements: Must hold a baccalaureate or higher degree in nursing. Must have completed a practice requirement in school nursing that can be met by completion of a two-hundred-hour supervised college-sponsored internship or practicum in school nursing, or completion of 1,500 hours in school nursing practice, education supervision, or direction of other persons engaged in school nursing within the past three years, or a combination of practicum hours and school nursing experience.

School Nurse Practitioner*

Title Awarded: CS

Requirements: Must hold a master's or higher degree in nursing. Must have been prepared as a school nurse practitioner (SNP) in either an SNP graduate nursing degree program or a formal postgraduate SNP track or program granting graduate-level academic credit.

From *AJNCareer Guide*, 1997, Part II; 97(1): pages 19–25. Reprinted with permission of Lippincott-Raven Publishers.
*Has met the standards of the American Board of Nursing Specialties, a national peer review program.
†Only COHN-S, not COHN, is approved by the American Board of Nursing Specialties.

APPENDIX

HOW TO GET A LICENSE

This appendix provides complete details about certification and licensure. As you can see, there is quite a variation in fees, time requirements, and so forth from state to state, so it is important that you check out the licensure information that applies to any state in which you desire to practice. For example, while most states have a biennial licensure period, Connecticut has an annual licensure period and Iowa has a triannual period. Such variations apply all the way down the line: fees, time limits, continuing education requirements, and so forth. So, we repeat, be certain to check the licensure information for any state in which you wish to practice. It will help you in deciding on the location that best matches your career accomplishments and objectives.

Board of Nursing	Licensing Period	Fees — Exam	Fees — Endorsement	Fees — Renewal	Temporary Permit — Fee	Temporary Permit — Time Limit	Limitations on Reexamination	Continuing Education Requirements
Alabama Board of Nursing RSA Plaza, Ste. 250 770 Washington Ave. Montgomery, AL 36130-3900 (334) 242-4060	Biennial Dec. 31, even year (R.N.) odd year (L.P.N.)	$85 (R.N.) $75 (L.P.N.) (NCLEX fee not included)	$80 (R.N.) $70 (L.P.N.) $100 C.R.N.P., C.R.N.A., C.N.M.) $50 temp. license	$60 (R.N., L.P.N.); $50 (C.R.N.P., C.R.N.A., C.N.M.)	$50 examination (R.N., L.P.N.)	90 days following graduation; 3 months if by endorsement	no limit	24 hours per renewal period
Alaska Board of Nursing Dept. of Commerce Div. of Occupational Licensing P.O. Box 110806 Juneau, AK 99811 (907) 465-2534	Biennial Nov. 30, even year (R.N.) Biennial Sept. 30, even year (L.P.N.)	$155 (NCLEX fee not included)	$155	$105	$50	4 months if by endorsement; permit by exam	must pass within 5 years; then only with remediation	2 of the 3 required for license renewal: • 30 contact hours of CE • 30 hours of profession- al nursing activities • 320 hours of nursing employment
Arizona Board of Nursing 1651 E. Morten Ave. Ste. 150 Phoenix, AZ 85020 (602) 331-8111	Biennial birthdate	$135 $88 ETS exam	$70 (R.N.) $100 (A.P.N. and C.N.S.)	$50 (R.N.)	$25	2 months if by endorsement; no permit by exam	4 times within 1 year	none
Arkansas State Board of Nursing Univ. Tower Bldg. 1123 S. Univ. Ave. Ste. 800 Little Rock, AR 72204 (501) 686-2700	Biennial birthdate	$55 (C.A.F.N.S.) (NCLEX fee not included)	$75 (R.N., L.P.N.)	$40	$10	up to 90 days if by endorsement and advanced practice; no permit by exam	no limit	none
California Board of Registered Nursing 400 R St. Ste. 4030 Sacramento, CA 95814 (916) 322-3350	Biennial last day of month following birth month	$75 application fee; $32 finger- print fee; $88 ETS exam ($97.25 by mail)	$50 endorse- ment fee; $56 finger- print fee; $60 endorsement to other states	$80	$30 interim permit $30 temporary license	pending results of first exam; 6 months if by endorsement	no limit	all R.N.s 30 contact hours every 2 years

Board of Nursing	Licensing Period	Fees				Temporary Permit		Limitations on Reexamination	Continuing Education Requirements
		Exam	Endorsement	Renewal		Fee	Time Limit		

Board of Nursing	Licensing Period	Exam	Endorsement	Renewal	Fee	Time Limit	Limitations on Reexamination	Continuing Education Requirements
Colorado Board of Nursing 1560 Broadway Ste. 880 Denver, CO 80202 (303) 894-2430	Biennial Sept. 30 (R.N., even and odd years); June 30 (L.P.N., even years)	(NCLEX fee not included) $71 (R.N.) $51 (L.P.N.)	$81 (R.N.) $61 (L.P.N.)	$100 (R.N.) $73 (L.P.N.)	included in application fee	90 days; 4 months if by endorsement	no limit	none
Connecticut Dept. of Public Health Nurse Licensure 410 Capitol Ave. MS # 12APP P.O. Box 340308 Hartford, CT 06134-0308 (860) 509-7570/71/73	Annual last day of birth month	$90 (R.N.) (NCLEX fee not included) $75 (L.P.N.)	$90 (R.N.) $75 (L.P.N.)	$50 (R.N.) $30 (L.P.N.)	included in application fee	90 days from completion of nursing program. Temporary permit also available for endorsement applicants, valid for 120 days, nonrenewable, must hold valid license in another state	may test no more than once every 91 days and no more than 4 times in 1 year	none
Delaware Board of Nursing 861 Silver Lake Blvd. Cannon Bldg. Ste. 203 Dover, DE 19904	Biennial Feb. 28, May 31, Sept. 30, odd year; depending on license number (R.N.); Feb. 28, even year (L.P.N.)	$84 first time (as of 7/94) $10 re-examination (NCLEX fee not included)	$84	$74	included in licensure fee	90 days from date of graduation pending results of first exam; endorsement applicants must hold valid license in another state; renewable up to 6 months	unlimited number of times within 2 years, 1 year re-exams	nurses not actively employed in past 5 years must provide evidence of satisfactory completion of refresher program within past 2 years, must have 1,000 hours employment in past 5 years to renew or 400 hours of practice; 30 contact hours every 2 years for R.N.; 24 contact hours for L.P.N.

Board of Nursing	Licensing Period	Fees				Temporary Permit		Limitations on Reexamination	Continuing Education Requirements
		Exam	Endorsement	Renewal		Fee	Time Limit		
District of Columbia Nurses Examining Board 614 H Street, NW Room 904 Washington, DC 20001 (202) 727-7454/7461	Biennial	$50	$40	$48		none	none	no limit	applicants for reinstatement of license must submit 12 contact hours for each year after 6/30/90 that applicant was not licensed, up to a maximum of 24 contact hours
Florida Board of Nursing 4080 Woodcock Dr. Ste. 202 Jacksonville, FL 32207 (904) 858-6940	Biennial Apr. 30 or July 31, even year; Apr. 30, odd year (R.N.); July 31, odd year (L.P.N.)	$160 (NCLEX fee not included)	$175	$65		included in licensure fee	pending results of first exam, up to 60 days; 60 days plus active license if by endorsement; staggered renewal cycles	3 times, then must take remediation	3 hours HIV/AIDS training for initial licensure; 25 contact hours every biennial renewal period, including 1 hour HIV/AIDS and 1 hour domestic violence; ARNPs may earn up to 50 percent of CE requirement as CME credit
Georgia Board of Nursing 237 Coliseum Dr. Macon, Georgia 30303 (912) 207-1640	Biennial Jan. 31, odd year	$88 NCLEX (plus $9.25 when registering by telephone) $40 exam fee	$60	$60 ($40 if paid before 11/30)		included in application fee	6 months if by endorsement; no permit by exam; provisional authority to practice may be issued to eligible A.P.R.N. graduates	every 91 days within 3-year period from date of graduation (or date of eligibility for out-of-country graduates)	none (R.N.s) A.P.R.N.s must meet recertification requirements, which include continuing education
Hawaii Hawaii Board of Nursing P.O. Box 3469 Honolulu, HI 96801 (808) 586-3000	Biennial June 30, odd year	$88 (R.N. and L.P.N.) (Application fee $20)	Fees vary depending on year license is issued. Noted on application information sheet. ($70/$115)	$90		none	repealed	every 90 days	A.P.R.N.s must meet recertification requirements including CE

Board of Nursing	Licensing Period	Fees			Temporary Permit		Limitations on Reexamination	Continuing Education Requirements
		Exam	Endorsement	Renewal	Fee	Time Limit		
Idaho Board of Nursing 280 N. 8th St., Ste. 210 P.O. Box 83720 Boise, ID 83720-0061 (208) 334-3110	Biennial Aug. 31, odd year	$75	$75	$45	$15	90 days	no limit	A.P.R.N.s 30 contact hours each renewal period
Illinois Dept. of Professional Regulation, 3rd Fl. 320 W. Washington St. Springfield, IL 62786	Biennial May 31, even year (R.N.); Jan. 31, odd year (L.P.N.)	$50 licensure fee (NCLEX fee not included)	$50	$40	$25	6 months	3 years	none
Indiana State Board of Nursing Health Professions Bureau, Room 041 402 W. Washington St. Indianapolis, IN 46204	Biennial Oct. 31, odd year	$30 (R.N.) (NCLEX fee not included) $20 (P.N.)	In: $30 Out: $10	$17	$10	90 days if by endorsement; no temporary permit for exam candidates	no limit; may retest every 90 days	none
Iowa Board of Nursing 400 SW 8th St., Ste. B Des Moines, IA 50319 (515) 281-3255	Triennial birth month	$75 (R.N. and L.P.N.)	$101	$81 (R.N. and L.P.N.) $63 A.R.N.P.	included in application fee	30 days if by endorsement; no temporary permit for licensure exam	no limit	all R.N.s and L.P.N.s 45 contact hours every 3 years
Kansas State Board of Nursing Landon State Office Bldg. 900 SW Jackson Ste. 551 S. Topeka, KS 66612-1230 (785) 296-4929	Biennial birthdate	$70 (R.N.) $45 (L.P.N.)	$70 (R.N.) $45 (L.P.N.)	$50 (R.N., R.N.A., and L.P.N.) $20 (A.R.N.P.)	$40 (A.R.N.P. initial application); $10 (A.R.N.P. permit); $75 R.N.A.); $90 (R.N.A. permit)	pending results of first exam, or no longer than 120 days; 120 days if by endorsement	petition board to retake examination if longer than 20 months after graduation	all R.N.s and L.P.N.s 30 contact hours every every 2 years
Kentucky Board of Nursing 312 Whittington Pwy. Ste. 300 Louisville, KY 40222-5172 (502) 329-7000	Biennial Oct. 31, even year (R.N. and A.R.N.P.); odd year (L.P.N.)	$80 (R.N. and L.P.N.)	$80 (R.N.) $160 (A.R.N.P.) $50 (S.A.N.E.)	$65 active (R.N.) $45 inactive $55 (A.R.N.P.) $40 (S.A.N.E.)	included in application fee (R.N. and (A.R.N.P.)	6 months if by endorsement; for A.R.N.P.s, may vary depending on individual type; no temporary permit for new graduates	may retest every 91 days	all R.N.s and L.P.N.s 30 contact hours every 2 years; 2 of the 30 hours must be AIDS CE-approved by the Kentucky Cabinet for Human Resources; for A.R.N.P.s, 5 of the 30 hours must be pharmacology CE; S.A.N.E.s must have 5 of 30 hours in a related field

Board of Nursing	Licensing Period	Fees Exam	Fees Endorsement	Fees Renewal	Temporary Permit Fee	Temporary Permit Time Limit	Limitations on Reexamination	Continuing Education Requirements
Louisiana Board of Nursing 3510 Causeway Blvd. Ste. 501 Metairie, LA 70002 (504) 838-5332	Annual Jan. 31	$80 (NCLEX fee not included)	In: $100 (R.N.); $100 (A.P.R.N.) Out: $25	$45 (R.N.) $50 (A.P.R.N.)	included in application fee	pending results of first exam; 90 days if by endorsement	4 times within 4 years after graduation	all R.N.s must have 5, 10, or 15 contact hours every year, based on employment
Maine Board of Nursing 24 Stone St. State House Station 158 Augusta, ME 04333 (207) 287-1133	Biennial birthdate	$60 (R.N.) $50 (L.P.N.) $25 (A.P.R.N.)	$60 (R.N.) $50 (L.P.N.) $25 (A.P.R.N.)	$40 $25 (A.P.R.N.)	included in application fee	90 days if by endorsement; no permit for L.P.N./R.N. exam candidates; provisional authorization may be issued to eligible A.P.R.N. graduates	no limit; may retest every 91 days	none: R.N.s and L.P.N.s A.P.R.N.s must meet recertification requirements, which include 75 CEUs in specialty area within 2-year period of licensure
Maryland Board of Nursing 4140 Patterson Ave. Baltimore, MD 21215 (410) 585-1900	Annual birth month	$50	$75	$30	$25	90 days, not renewable; no graduate nurse status	no limit	none
Massachusetts Board of Registration in Nursing 239 Causeway St. Boston, MA 02114 (617) 727-9961	Biennial birthdate even year (R.N.) odd year (L.P.N.)	$166 (R.N.) (NCLEX fee included) $166 (L.P.N.)	$75	$40	none	no graduate nurse status	no limit	all R.N.s and L.P.N.s 15 contact hours every 2 years
Michigan Board of Nursing P.O. Box 30670 Lansing, MI 48909 (517) 335-0918	Biennial Mar. 31	$120 (R.N.) $40 license fee $120 (L.P.N.)	$40	$40	none	no graduate nurse status	3 years or maximum of 6 times, whichever is sooner	25 hours every 2 years
Minnesota Board of Nursing 2829 University Ave., SE #500 Minneapolis, MN 55414 (612) 617-2270	Biennial birth month	$100	$100	$70 (late fee $50)	$50: exam $0: endorsement	60 days; 12 months if by endorsement	no limit	R.N.s 24 contact hours, L.P.N.s 12 contact hours every 2 years

Board of Nursing	Licensing Period	Fees Exam	Fees Endorsement	Fees Renewal	Temporary Permit Fee	Temporary Permit Time Limit	Limitations on Reexamination	Continuing Education Requirements
Mississippi Board of Nursing 1935 Lakeland, Ste. B Jackson, MS 39216 (601) 987-4188	Biennial Dec. 31 even year (R.N.) odd year (L.P.N.)	$60 (R.N. and L.P.N.)	$60 (R.N. and L.P.N.) $100 (N.P.)	$50 (R.N. and L.P.N.) $100 (N.P.)	$25 $100 (N.P.)	90 days by endorsement; N.P.s, 120 days	no limit	N.P.s 40 hours every 2 years
Missouri Board of Nursing P.O. Box 656 3605 Missouri Blvd. Jefferson City, MO 65102 (573)751-0681	Annual Apr. 30 (R.N.) May 31 (L.P.N.)	$20 (R.N.) $11 (L.P.N.)	$30 (R.N.) $26 (L.P.N.)	$46 (R.N.) $38 (L.P.N.)	included in application fee	6 months	no limit	none
Montana Board of Nursing Arcade Bldg. 111 N. Jackson P.O. Box 200513 Helena, MT 59620-0513 (406) 444-2071	Annual Dec. 31	$70	$70	$40	included in application fee	90 days, A.P.R.N.s, until results of first certifying exam	no limit	none; A.P.R.N.s, for prescriptive authority, 6 hours pharmacology per renewal period
Nebraska Board of Nursing P.O. Box 94986 Lincoln, NE 68509 (402) 471-4376	Biennial even year	$76 or $77 depending on year $200 (A.R.N.P.)	same	$42 $250 (A.R.N.P.)	included in application fee	after passing exam for 60 days pending completion of application; 60 days if by endorsement	no limit	all R.N.s 500 hours of practice plus 20 contact hours or 75 contact hours within preceding 5 years
Nevada Board of Nursing P.O. Box 46886 Las Vegas, NV 89114 (702) 486-5800	Biennial birthdate	$100 (R.N.) $90 (L.P.N.)	$100 (R.N.) $95 (L.P.N.) $200 (A.P.N.) $200 (C.R.N.A.)	$100 (R.N. and L.P.N.) $200 (A.P.N.) $200 (C.R.N.A.)	included in application fee; $50 if not seeking permanent license (R.N. and L.P.N.)	4 months, not renewable in 12-month period (R.N. and L.P.N.)	4 times, then only with remediation after the 2nd attempt (R.N. and L.P.N.)	all licensed nurses 30 contact hours every 2 years at renewal; N.P.s and C.R.N.A.s additional 15 contact hours

Board of Nursing	Licensing Period	Fees			Temporary Permit		Limitations on Reexamination	Continuing Education Requirements
		Exam	Endorsement	Renewal	Fee	Time Limit		
New Hampshire Board of Nursing P.O. Box 3898 Concord, NH 03302-3898 (603) 271-2323	Biennial birthdate	$80	$70	$60	$20	180 days or until results of first exam are received and license issued	no limit	active in practice; 900 hours using nursing knowledge, judgment, and skills within 4 years immediately prior to application for renewal, endorsement, and reinstatement, and 30 contact hours every 2 years
New Jersey Board of Nursing P.O. Box 45010 Newark, NJ 07101 (201) 504-6430	Biennial Mar. 31	$140 (R.N. and L.P.N.)	$140 (R.N. and L.P.N.)	$65	no temporary license	30 hours remediation after 3rd failure	no limit	advance practice 30 contact hours every 2 years
New Mexico Board of Nursing 4206 Louisiana NE Ste. A Albuquerque, NM 87109 (505) 841-8340	Biennial	$90 (R.N. and L.P.N.)	$90 (R.N. and L.P.N.)	$60 (R.N. and L.P.N.)	included in application fee; must have NM employment verified	24 weeks from graduation if complete application process within 12 weeks of graduation; 6 months if by endorsement	no limit	all licensed nurses 30 contact hours every 2 years; N.P.s 50 contact hours, which includes 15 hours minimum in pharmacology every 2 years
New York Board for Nursing State Ed. Dept. Cultural Education Center Albany, NY 12230 (518) 474-3843	Triennial (licensed as of 9/1/83)	$120 (includes first license and 3-year registration (for R.N. and L.P.N.)	$120	$50	$35	10 days after exam scores posted, or up to 1 year	no limit	one-time requirement for registration; 2-hour course on child abuse; 4-hour course in infection control every 4 years
North Carolina Board of Nursing P.O. Box 2129 Raleigh, NC 27602 (919) 782-3211	Biennial birthdate	$50 (R.N. and L.P.N.) (NCLEX fee not included)	$105	$60	included in application fee	6 months, not renewable	no limit	none

Board of Nursing	Licensing Period	Fees Exam	Fees Endorsement	Fees Renewal	Temporary Permit Fee	Temporary Permit Time Limit	Limitations on Reexamination	Continuing Education Requirements
North Dakota Board of Nursing 919 S. 7th St. Ste. 504 Bismarck, ND 58504-5881 (701) 328-9777	Biennial	$75	$75	$60 (R.N.) $50 (L.P.N.)	included in application fee	90 days pending results of first exam or by endorsement	5 attempts in 3 years	nursing practice for relicensure must meet or exceed 500 hours within preceding 5 years
Ohio Board of Nursing 77 South High St. Ste. 400 Columbus, OH 43215 (614) 466-3947	Biennial Sept. 1, odd year	$50	$50	$35	included in endorsement application fee	endorsement—4 months	no limit; must wait 3 months	24 hours for R.N. and L.P.N. in a 2-year period
Oklahoma Board of Nursing 2915 Classen Blvd. Ste. 524 Oklahoma City, OK 73106 (405) 962-1800	Biennial birthdate	$75	$75	$60	included in application fee	90 days if by endorsement	no limit for NCLEX	none
Oregon Board of Nursing 800 NE Oregon St. Ste. 465 Portland, OR 97232 (503) 731-4745	Biennial birthdate	$80	$115	$65 R.N. and L.P.N. $105 N.P.	none		3 years past graduation for U.S. graduates; 3 years past application for R.N.s from other countries	R.N., N.P., L.P.N.: 960 hours of practice within past 5 years. N.P.s: 100 clock hours of continuing education every 2 years
Pennsylvania Board of Nursing P.O. Box 2649 Harrisburg, PA 17105-2649 (717) 783-7142	Biennial	$35 board $88 NCLEX	$25	$16 (P.R.) $21 (R.N.) $26 (C.R.N.P.)	$20	1 year maximum; examination results preempt permit	no limit	none
Rhode Island Board of Nurse Registration and Nurse Education Three Capitol Hill Cannon Bldg., Room 105 Providence, RI 02908 (401)277-5700	Biennial Mar. 1 by license number odd/even	$75 board $88 NCLEX	$75 (R.N.) $50 (L.P.N.)	$50	none	pending results of first exam but no longer than 90 days after graduation; 90 days if by endorsement	up to 4 times per year, but not more often than once in any 3-month period	none

Board of Nursing	Licensing Period	Fees			Temporary Permit		Limitations on Reexamination	Continuing Education Requirements
		Exam	Endorsement	Renewal	Fee	Time Limit		
South Carolina Board of Nursing 110 Centerview Dr. Ste. 202 P.O. Box 12367 Columbia, SC 29211 (803) 896-4550	Annual Oct. 1–Jan. 31	$65 (R.N.) $45 (L.P.N.)	$75	$32	no temporary permit	pending results of first exam; 8 weeks if by endorsement	up to 4 times in 1 year, then must remediate	minimum practice requirement 960 hours in preceding 5 years
South Dakota Board of Nursing 3307 South Lincoln Sioux Falls, SD 57105-5224 (605) 335-4973	Biennial birthdate	$60 board $88 ETS	$75	$55 (includes $10 for nurse education assistance loan fund)	$15	pending results of first exam; 90 days if by endorsement	maximum of 4 times per year in 3 years postgraduation, then must requalify	continuing practice requirement 140 hours/year or 480 hours/6 years
Tennessee Board of Nursing 283 Plus Park Blvd. Nashville, TN 37247-1010 (615) 367-6232	Biennial birthdate/birth year	$75 plus $88 NCLEX	$85	$50	$15	6 months by endorsement	no limit	continuous practice requirement
Texas Board of Nurse Examiners Box 140466 Austin, TX 78714 (512) 835-4880	Biennial birthdate odd/even year	$50 board $88 NCLEX	$75 (includes temporary license)	$35 (includes $5 for peer assistance)	$15	6 months to allow nurse to satisfy requirement	3 attempts within 4 years	20 contact hours for 2 years
Utah Board of Nursing Division of Professional Licensing 160 E. 300 South P.O.Box 45805 Salt Lake City, UT 84145	Biennial Jan. 31 odd year	$88	$50	$50		no temporary licenses	those who fail to pass NCLEX exam within 2 years after completing educational program must submit plan of action for approval before retaking	have practiced not less than 400 hours during 2 years preceding application for renewal; or have completed 30 contact hours or have practiced not less than 200 hours and completed 15 contact hours during 2 years preceding application for renewal

Board of Nursing	Licensing Period	Fees Exam	Fees Endorsement	Fees Renewal	Temporary Permit Fee	Temporary Permit Time Limit	Limitations on Reexamination	Continuing Education Requirements
Vermont Board of Nursing 109 State St. Montpelier, VT 05609-1106 (802) 828-2396	Biennial (R.N. licensed as of 3/31/95 odd year; L.P.N. 1/31/96)	$110 board $88 ETS	$60	$35 + $5 surcharge	none	pending receipt of examination results or 90 days, whichever comes first	2 times, then need board nursing approval	none
Virginia Board of Nursing 6606 W. Broad St., 4th Floor Richmond, VA 23230-1717 (804) 662-9909	Biennial birthdate/birth year	$25	$50	$40	none	pending results of first exam; 30 days if by endorsement	no limit	none
Washington Nursing Commission P.O. Box 1099 Olympia, WA 98507-1099 (360) 753-2686	Annual birthdate	$40 commission $88 ETS (NCLEX)	$40	$35	none	no permit	3 times in 2 years; then must requalify	advanced registered nurse practitioner; 30 contact hours every 2 years with prescriptive authorization; 15 added hours in pharmacology as of 1/1/87
West Virginia Board of Examiners for R.N.s 101 Dee Dr. Charleston, WV 25311-1620 (304) 558-3596	Annual Dec. 31	$51.50 $40 NCLEX	$30	$25	$10	pending results of first exam but no longer than 90 days from graduation, new graduates only; 90 days if by endorsement	2 times, then additional requirements	implementation in 1997
Wisconsin Board of Nursing P.O. Box 8935 Madison, WI 53708 (608) 266-0257	Biennial Mar. 1, even year (R.N.); May 1 odd year (L.P.N.)	$40 + $88 test service (R.N.) $40 + $88 test service (R.N.)	$50	$40 (R.N. and L.P.N.)	$10	3 months upon proof of graduation; 3 months if by endorsement; must take exam before expiration to maintain eligibility	no limit	none

Board of Nursing	Licensing Period	Fees			Temporary Permit		Limitations on Reexamination	Continuing Education Requirements
		Exam	Endorsement	Renewal	Fee	Time Limit		
Wyoming Board of Nursing Barrett Bldg. 2nd Floor 2301 Central Ave. Cheyenne, WY 82002 (307) 777-7601	Biennial June 30 even year	$80 (R.N. and L.P.N.) $88 NCLEX	$100 (R.N.) $90 (L.P.N.)	$65 (R.N.) $55 (L.P.N.)	included in application fee	90 days from date of issue	3 times, then only with remediation	none

BIBLIOGRAPHY

BOOKS

Birchenall, Joan M., and Mary Eileen Streight. *Health Occupations: Explorations and Career Planning.* St. Louis, MO: C.V. Mosby Co., 1989.

Bullough, Vernon, et al. *Florence Nightingale and Her Era: A Collection of New Scholarship.* New York: Garland Publishing Co., 1990.

Camenson, Blythe. "Registered Nurses," in *On the Job: Real People Working in Health Careers.* Chicago: VGM Career Books, 1996.

Carnegie, M. Elizabeth. *The Path We Travel: Blacks in Nursing, 1854–1990.* New York: National League for Nursing, 1991.

Donahue, M. P. *Nursing: The Finest Act: An Illustrated History.* New York: Abrams, 1986.

Frederickson, Keville. *Opportunities in Nursing Careers.* Chicago: VGM Career Books, 2003.

Haase, Patricia T. *The Origins and Rise of the Associate Degree in Nursing Education.* Durham, NC: Duke University, 1990.

Henderson, V. A. *Basic Principles of Nursing Care.* London: International Council of Nurses, 1961.

Heron, Jackie. *Exploring Careers in Nursing.* New York: Rosen Publishing Group, 1990.

Hill, Signe, and Helen F. Howlett. *Success in Practical Nursing*, 3rd edition. Philadelphia: Saunders, 1997.

Jones, Anne Hudson. *Badges of Nurses: Perspectives from History, Art, and Literature.* Philadelphia: University of Pennsylvania Press, 1982.

Kacen, Alex. "A Look at Two Physician Extenders—the Physician Assistant and the Nurse Practitioner." *Opportunities in Paramedical Careers.* Chicago: VGM Career Books, 1994.

Kelly, Lucie. *Dimensions of Professional Nursing,* 7th edition. New York: McGraw-Hill, 1995.

Kraegel, Janet M., and Mary Kachoyeanos. *Just a Nurse: From Clinic to Hospital Battleground to Cancer Unit.* New York: Dell, 1989.

National League for Nursing. *Scholarships and Loans for Nursing Education, 1996–1997.* New York: National League for Nursing, 1997.

Nightingale, Florence. *Notes on Nursing: What It Is and What It Is Not.* London: Harrison & Sons (facsimile edition), J. B. Lippincott Co., 1946.

NLN Center for Research in Nursing Education and Community. *NLN Guide to Undergraduate R.N. Education.* New York: National League for Nursing, 1996.

Robinson, Alice, and Mary Freres. *Your Future in a Nursing Career.* New York: Rosen Press, 1978.

Rogers, Carla S., Ph.D. *How to Get into the Right Nursing Program.* Chicago: VGM Career Books, 1997.

Swanson, Barbara. *Careers in Health Care.* Chicago: VGM Career Books, 1995.

Wright, John. *The American Almanac of Jobs and Salaries 1997–1998.* New York: Avon Books, 1996.

PAMPHLETS AND REPORTS

Advanced Practice Nurses. Chicago: Encyclopedia of Careers, 2001.

Advanced Practice Nursing: A New Age in Health Care. Washington, D.C.: American Nurses Association, 1993.

Anesthetics . . . Certified Nurse Anesthetists. Park Ridge, IL: American Association of Nurse Anesthetists, 1994.

Education Programs Accredited by the American College of Nurse-Midwives. Washington, D.C.: Division of Accreditation, American College of Nurse-Midwives, 1993.

Fact Sheet: Certified Nurse-Midwives: Careers and Background. Washington, D.C.: American College of Nurse-Midwives, 1993.

Facts: American College of Nurse-Midwives. Medicine's Historical Answer to Maternal Health Problems. Washington, D.C.: American College of Nurse-Midwives, 1993.

Fowkes, Virginia K., Nona N. Gamel, Sandra R. Wilson, and Ronald G. Garcia. *Effectiveness of Educational Strategies Preparing Physician Assistants, Nurse Practitioners and Certified Nurse-Midwives.* Public Health Reports, U.S. Department of Health and Human Services, v. 108, no. 5, October 1994.

"Licensed Practical Nurses." *Occupational Outlook Handbook, 1996–1997.* Washington, D.C.: U.S. Department of Labor, 208–209.

Managed Care: Challenges and Opportunities for Nursing. Washington, D.C.: American Nurses Association, 1995.

Midwives: Basic Facts about Certified Nurse-Midwives. Washington, D.C.: American College of Nurse-Midwives, 1993.

The Nurse Practitioner: A Primary Health Care Practitioner. Austin, TX: American Academy of Nurse Practitioners, 1988.

Nurse Practitioners. Moravia, NY: Chronicle Guidance Publications, Inc., 1993.

Nurses Renew Push for Passage of Nursing Shortage Legislation. Washington, D.C.: American Nurses Association, December 4, 2001.

Nurse Practitioners, Physician Assistants & Certified Nurse-Midwives: A Policy Analysis. HCS37. U.S. Congress: Office of Technology Assessment, December 1986.

Nursing Quality Indicators for Acute Care Settings & ANA's Safety & Quality Initiative. Washington, D.C.: American Nurses Association, 1996.

Primary Health Care: The Nurse Solution. Washington, D.C.: American Nurses Association, 1993.

Registered Nurse: A Distinctive Health Care Profession. Washington, D.C.: American Nurses Association, 1993.

The Registered Nurse Population: Findings from the National Survey of Registered Nurses, March 1988. U.S. Department of Health and Human Services, Bureau of Health, Division of Nursing, June 1990.

"Registered Nurses." *Occupational Outlook Handbook, 2000–2001.* Washington, D.C.: U.S. Department of Labor, 210–13.

"Registered Nurses." *Chicago: Encyclopedia of Careers and Vocational Guidance,* 366–69.

Scope of Practice for Nurse Practitioners. Austin, TX: American Academy of Nurse Practitioners, 1992.

Standards of Clinical Nursing Care. Washington, D.C.: American Nurses Association, 1991.

"Testimony of the American Nurses Association Before Committee on Health, Education, Labor & Pensions on Direct Care Staffing Shortages." Washington, D.C.: American Nurses Association, May 17, 2001.

Today's Certified Nurse-Midwife. Washington, D.C.: American College of Nurse-Midwives, 1992.

Today's Registered Nurse: Numbers and Demographics. Washington, D.C.: American Nurses Association, 1996.

Towers, Jan. "Report of the U.S. Survey of the American Academy of Nurse Practitioners. Academy of Nurse Practitioners: Part V—Comparison of Nurse Practitioners to Practice Settings." *Journal of the American Academy of Nurse Practitioners*, January–March 1991.

ARTICLES

American Nurses Association. "The American Nurse. Managed Care: Does the Promise Meet the Potential?" American Nurses Association, 1995.

Bailey, A. K. Hallam, and K. Hurst. "Triage on Trial," *Nursing Times* 13, no. 44 (1987): 65.

Bennett, Jane. "New Choices in Who Cares for You," *Kiplinger's Personal Finance Magazine* 47, no. 11 (1993): 124.

Bezyack, Mary Anne K. "Advanced Practice: Is It Right for You?" *American Journal of Nursing, Part II*, 96 (January 1996): 15.

Bower, Kathleen A. "Case Management by Nurses," *American Nurses Publishing* 83, no. 49 (1987): 65.

Caliafano, Jr., Joseph A. "Nurse Practitioners: Breaking the Physician's Health Care Monopoly," *American Journal of Nursing* 95 (June 1995): 16B–16D.

Carruthers, Evaylyn P. "Nursing," *Encarta '97 Encyclopedia*, Microsoft Corp., 1997.

Chatz, Vera. "Nursing in the '90s: Profession Has Changed Since Nightingale Era," *Chicago Sun-Times*, 4 May 1992: 3, 14.

Cullen, Allethaire. "Burnout: Why Blame the Nurse," *American Journal of Nursing* 95, no. 11 (1995): 23–27.

Culley, Joan M., Janet A. Courtney, and Lisa M. Diamond. "A Continuing Education Program to Retrain Registered Nurses," *The Journal of Continuing Education in Nursing* 27 (November–December 1996).

Cyr, J. P. "Males in Nursing," *Nursing Management* 23, no. 7 (1992): 54.

DeLaFuente, Della. "Special Delivery: Comfort Factor Draws More Women to Licensed Midwives," *Chicago Sun-Times*, 6 (November 1995): 47.

Emmett, Arielle. "Health Care Trends That Will Reshape Nursing," *Nursing* (November 1994).

Ferazzy, Mary Anne, Mary Le Page, Marianne Fightlin, H. Hunter Hadsfield, and Catherine D. DeAngelis. "Nurse Practitioner Redux Revisited," *Journal of the American Medical Association* 272, no. 8 (1994): 591.

"Filling the Gap," *Modern Health Care* 21, no. 19 (1991): 21–24.

Fitzgerald, Margaret, P. Eugene Jones, Burton Lazar, Martin McHugh, and Christopher Wang. "The Mid-Level Provider: Colleague or Competitor," *Patient Care* 29, no. 1 (1995): 20.

Fondiller, Shirley H., and Barbara J. Nerone. "Preparing for Nursing's Future," *American Journal of Nursing* 96, no. 9 (1996): 16F–16G.

Grust, Sayville. "Hospital Horrors," *American Journal of Nursing* 97, no. 1 (1997): 16.

"How to Get the Job You Want" (Career Planning for Nurses). *Nursing Times*, v. 97, no. 35 (August 30, 2001).

"Huge Job Loss Projections Shock Health Professionals," *American Journal of Nursing* 96, no. 1 (1996): 61.

Joel, Lucille A. "The CNS and NP Roles: Controversy and Conflict," *American Journal of Nursing* 95, no. 4 (1995): 7.

Joel, Lucille A. "Hallmarks of a Good Practice Setting," *American Journal of Nursing* (Career Guide), Part II, 96 (January 1996): 3.

Joel, Lucille A. "Map a New Course for Your Career," *American Journal of Nursing* (Career Guide), Part II, 96 (January 1996): 8.

Johnson, G. "Men in Nursing," *Nursing Outlook* 42, no. 5 (1994): 244.

Kassirer, Jerome E. "What Role for Nurse Practitioners in Primary Care," *New England Journal of Medicine* 330, no. 3 (1994): 204.

Khanna, Prema. "While Physician Extenders Proliferate, Doctors Worry About Competition," *Wall Street Journal*, 9 August 1992.

"Labor & Delivery Nursing." *Nursing 2001*, December 2001.

La Pointe, Sylvia. "Nursing in the Armed Forces," *American Journal of Nursing* (Career Guide), Part II, 96 (1996): 150.

Letizia, B. "Ban on Male Nurses in Labor and Delivery Is Upheld," *RN* 512, no. 12 (1994): 16.

Lokos, Connie. "Advanced Practice Nurses," *Nursing Homes* (March 1996).

"L.P.N.s Deserve Recognition," *American Journal of Nursing* 96, no. 9 (1996): 16.

Mantel, Donna Lee. "Off Duty Doesn't Mean Off the Hook." *RN* v. 62, no. 10, p. 71–72.

"Midwives Make Sense If We Trust Our Bodies," *Chicago Sun-Times*, 13 November 1995.

Mills, Claire. "On Her Own," *RN* 555, no. 7 (1992): 28.

Monteague, Jim. "M.D.s Acknowledging the Value of Physician Extenders," *Hospitals and Health Networks* (1994).

"Notes from the National Sample Survey of Registered Nurses." Division of Nursing, HRSA, U.S. Department of Health and Human Services, July 2002.

"Nursing," *Encyclopedia Americana*. Danbury, CT: Grolier Inc., 1995.

Shindul-Rothschild, Judith, Diane Berry, and Ellen Long-Middleton. "Where Have All the Nurses Gone," *American Journal of Nursing* 96, no. 11 (1996): 25–39.

Sloan, Andrea. "Impaired Nurses: Reclaiming Careers," *RN* 64 (February 2001), pp. 58–64.

Soboloewski, Sally. "See You in Home Care," *American Journal of Nursing* (Career Guide), Part II, 96 (January 1996): 10.

"Spotlight on Nurse-Midwives," *Nursing 2001*, v. 32, no. 1.

Squires, Timothy E. "Men in Nursing," *RN* (July 1995): 26–28.

Thompson, Alicia. "The Art of Nursing," *School Library Journal*, v. 46, no. 9, p. 87.

ABOUT THE AUTHOR

Terry Sacks is an independent writer-editor with more than twenty-five years of experience in communications. During that period he has written dozens of news stories, magazine articles, and speeches, as well as several books. Sacks's articles have appeared in such publications as *LifeTime*, *Hospitals*, and *Chicago Medicine*.

Sacks, a graduate of Northwestern's Medill School of Journalism, has strong credentials in health and medical-related topics. For three years, from 1970 to 1973, he was director of communications for the Chicago Medical Society, the local professional group for physicians in Chicago and Cook County. He has also held positions in communications for the American Osteopathic Association, the American Association of Dental Schools, and several hospitals in Chicago.

Sacks is currently on the journalism faculty of Columbia College in Chicago, where he teaches "Introduction to Mass Media." At Columbia he has also taught courses in news reporting, feature writing, editing company publications, and history of journalism.

For the past fifteen years, Sacks has headed his own writing and communications firm, Terence J. Sacks Associates. He is active in the Independent Writers of Chicago (where he has also served on the board), the American Medical Writers Association, and the Publicity Club of Chicago.